A Guide to
Empirical Research
in Communication

To Laura and Tim,
who help me figure out things.

A Guide to
Empirical Research
in Communication
Rules for Looking

John Sumser

Sage Publications, Inc.
International Educational and Professional Publisher
Thousand Oaks ▪ London ▪ New Delhi

For information:

Sage Publications, Inc.
2455 Teller Road
Thousand Oaks, California 91320
E-mail: order@sagepub.com

Sage Publications Ltd.
6 Bonhill Street
London EC2A 4PU
United Kingdom

Sage Publications India Pvt. Ltd.
M-32 Market
Greater Kailash I
New Delhi 110 048 India

Printed in the United States of America

Library of Congress Cataloging-in-Publication Data

Sumser, John, 1948–
   A guide to empirical research in communication: Rules for looking /
by John Sumser.
      p.   cm.
   Includes bibliographical references and index.
   ISBN 0-7619-2222-9 (pbk.: alk. paper)
      1. Communication in the social sciences—Research.   2. Communication
in the social sciences—Methodology.   3. Social sciences—Research.
4. Social sciences—Methodology.   I. Title.
   H61.8 .S964   2000
   001.4′2—dc21   00-011029

01   02   03   04   05   06   07   7   6   5   4   3   2

Acquiring Editor:	Margaret H. Seawell
Editorial Assistant:	Heidi Van Middlesworth
Production Editor:	Diane S. Foster
Editorial Assistant:	Victoria Cheng
Typesetter:	Tina Hill
Cover Designer:	Michelle Lee

CONTENTS

ACKNOWLEDGMENTS

A number of students have helped me in the development of this manuscript. Their comments on clarity, examples, and grammar have been greatly appreciated. In particular, I would like to thank, in alphabetical order, Deolinda Brasil, Ashley Brown, Wendy Glaister, and Shannon Kerr.

I would also like to thank my editor, Margaret Seawell, and all the anonymous reviewers. Your comments and suggestions were tremendously helpful and strengthened the text. And finally, my gratitude goes to Elisabeth Magnus, my relentlessly observant copy editor, for her patience and professionalism.

PART I
THE CONCEPTS

1

WHAT IS SOCIAL SCIENCE RESEARCH METHODOLOGY?

In the social sciences, as in other human activities, we develop theories or explanations about the way the world is, and then we look to see if the world is in fact the way we have supposed. The problem, of course, is that we don't look at the world as neutral bystanders. We have interests, agendas, beliefs, values, hopes, social positions, and careers that combine with biases, wishful thinking, mistakes, faulty memories, and selective perceptions to make our observations about the world very questionable indeed.

Social science research methods are the rules of the game of "looking." By following these rules, we can know that we have drawn the clearest picture possible of the aspect of life that is being studied. Research methodology is the link between thinking and evidence. And we know, by how much other researchers follow these rules, just how much we can trust their conclusions.

This does not mean that the picture we have drawn is "true." *True* is not a word that is used much in research methodology. A clearly drawn picture of the world allows us to find our mistakes, and the mistakes of others, and to correct them if possible. A picture of the world drawn without regard for the Rules of Looking may be ultimately more accurate, but there is no way to know that: A letter from a friend may present the most accurate description of an aspect of social reality that has ever been written, but it does not allow us to ask, "How does she know that?" "What is the basis for these remarks?" "How much can I trust this picture, this explanation, of the world?"

IF NOT TRUTH, THEN WHAT?

> *For decades, scholars have struggled to divine from tiny teeth and bits of bone the ancient history of mammals, and despite the paucity of the fossil record paleontologists had pieced together a plausible account.*
>
> Yam (2000, p. 25)

Social scientists, like all scientists, are a cautious lot. And perhaps even more than physical scientists, social scientists are less interested in discovering *things* than in trying to determine the relationship *between* things. They are less concerned with *facts*, to put it another way, than with *explanations*.

The quote about paleontology that opened this section was included as an illustration of how cautious scientists can be. Look at the words that are used to introduce the *Scientific American* article on new thinking about the origins of mammals: *struggled, divine, pieced together, plausible.* All of these terms suggest the constant incompleteness of any kind of scientific inquiry. One frequently reads about the arrogance of science and scientists, but it should be recognized that scientists advance in tiny steps and are professionally committed to the idea that they may be wrong.[1] In fact, the possibility of being wrong is one of the anchors of science—it is what allows scientists to let go of the idea of truth.

If scientists are not looking for truth, what are they seeking? Answering this question raises a number of philosophical and ideological questions that are beyond the focus of this text, but some sort of answer is necessary. Scientists are seeking knowledge, but it is not so much knowledge about the world as it is knowledge about what happens when you look at the world. What a scientist knows is what scientists have found. What we know about communication—what we can claim to know as scholars, not what we feel is the truth as individuals—are the results of all the surveys, experiments, field studies, and content analysis projects that have been conducted in communication-related areas. Our knowledge is of what we have done, rather than knowledge of the world, of "the way things are." Because of this, we don't have one *plausible account* of human communication, we have a shifting and overlapping set of *plausible accounts* created by different theories, resulting in different tests. The idea of truth, in contrast, seems singular, final, and complete.

The Rules of Looking are agreed upon by those who make claims about the world. Ideally, these methods are designed to hold in check all of our biases, ideologies, and interests. And, to the extent that it is possible, they do so. Research methodology, however, is dependent on theory and conceptualizations. And theory and conceptualization are governed not by the Rules of Looking but by the Rules of Thinking—logic and grammar—and so are much more subject to individual and social perspectives. Because of this, research methodology—the Rules of Looking— will never present a complete picture of the way the world works, and we should neither want nor expect it to do so. Research methodology can force us to be honest in pursuit of our interests and to see clearly where we are wrong, where we agree, and where we disagree. It cannot, however, define our interests, perspectives, or values.

Social scientists, like all scientists, understand that their conclusions cannot be separated from the processes that created them. Before accepting any research conclusion, we need to know the data on which it is based, the way the important concepts were defined, and the rationale for the various decisions the researcher made. When we know these things, we can determine

how useful the research is to us, given our own purposes and
interests.

EMPIRICAL RESEARCH

The Rules of Looking govern what is called *empirical* research.
Research is empirical when the questions that one asks can most
appropriately be answered by looking at the world rather than by
thinking about it. That is, a question is empirical when the inquiry is governed by the Rules of Looking rather than the Rules of
Thinking.

The most famous story about this distinction is a very old one
involving an argument about the number of teeth in a horse's
mouth: A group of philosophers fiercely debated the question until a small child asked them why they didn't find a horse, open its
mouth, and count its teeth. The philosophers were treating an
empirical question as a conceptual, or logical, question.

This story is both illuminating and misleading. It is illuminating in that it points out an important distinction between empirical and theoretical activities. Without making this distinction,
the development of science and technology is not possible. Fur-
thermore, without this distinction, the ordinary lives of ordinary
people would become quite muddled. Daily problem solving
would break down in a muddle of philosophical thought. But the
example is also misleading because it makes the distinction seem
so obvious that only an idiot (or an intellectual) could fail to
make it correctly. And, as we'll see in the next section, this is not
the case.

THINKING AND LOOKING

*Without sensibility no object would be given to us, and without
the understanding no object would be thought. Thoughts
without content are empty: intuitions without concepts are*

blind. . . . The understanding is incapable of intuiting, and the
senses are incapable of thinking.

Kant, *Critique of Pure Reason,*
quoted in Coppleston (1960, p. 42)

In a congressional hearing on abortion in the late 1980s, a group of biologists were called in to determine precisely when "human life" begins. These "expert" witnesses were supposed to shed light on the human status of fetuses as if this status were an empirical, rather than a conceptual, problem. A far better group of "experts" would have consisted of theologians, philosophers, historians, and others who understood the history and the complexity of the idea of "humanity." When "human life" begins and ends is purely a matter of definition. At one point, not too long ago, women and children were not considered fully human (humanity was defined in terms of responsibility), and, of course, slave ownership was justified by the argument that slaves were not fully human. Nazis justified their killing of millions of people by simply denying that they were people—a tradition that is carried on today by skinheads and other bigots.

Congress was treating a question that could be solved only by *thinking* as if it were a question that could be solved by *looking*.

Questions about what we *should do* (about education, organizational structure, governmental policy, cultural directions, etc.) are also not empirical questions. Though empirical studies can help clarify the arguments—as they can clarify the arguments about who or what is "human"—the ultimate justifications are an intricate weave of ideas and values. The idea that "educational experts" can tell us what education is for or that social scientists can tell us what is the empirically correct way of thinking about sex or race or ecology involves a confusion no less serious than that which concerned the horse's teeth.

In real life, we approach the world with a mixture of empiricism and conceptualization because the two are inextricably linked. Immanuel Kant, the famous German philosopher, said that you cannot look at the world unless you have ideas and that

**SIDEBAR 1.1 The Relationship Between Thinking
                          and Looking**

In December 1997, astronomers detected the afterglow
of a cosmic blast, labeled GRB 971214, that occurred
some 12 billion years ago. According to researchers, the
explosion was so great that for a brief moment it out-
shone all the stars in the universe combined. Phil Ponce
(a reporter on Jim Lehrer's NewsHour) talks with Dr. David
Helfand (of Columbia University) about the big burst.

  Phil Ponce: And Professor, the $64,000 question: What
    caused it?
  David Helfand: What caused it? Yes, well, as I said, we've
    been waiting for 30 years to answer that question. And
    we've only taken the very first step along the road to the
    answer. There are about 150 separate theories that
    have been published for the origin of gamma ray bursts
    over the last 30 years. This destroys about 146 of them
    or so. But there are a few that are still viable. ("Fire in
    the Sky," 1998)

  A number of excellent books have been written showing
the social nature of science. Thomas Kuhn's famous *Structure of Scientific Revolutions* (1970) comes to mind, as does
Scientific Knowledge by Barnes, Bloor, and Henry (1996). At
the same time, however, only in the sciences could one
event force so many people to throw out ideas they had
spent a lifetime developing. Certainly, it is impossible to
imagine any event that would force religious or political lead-
ers to throw out their ideas and start over. And although
new information is capable of discounting theories in the
social sciences, I cannot think of anything that transformed
sociology or communication studies in the way that GRB
971214 transformed astronomy.
  Though most scientific revolutions are generated on the
thinking side, it is nice to know that looking can have such an
impact on ideas.

you cannot have ideas unless you look at the world. In this book, we are concerned with looking at the world, but we will also be talking continuously about conceptualization.

RESEARCH GOALS

People who have a naïve view of science—that it is the impersonal, atheoretical discovery of reality—can be disillusioned by the description provided here. Either scholarship leads to the truth, such people may say, or it is mere opinion, one no better than the other, regardless how fancy the language. But between truth and opinion is knowledge, and in the specialized version of knowledge that was described above there are guidelines for what counts and what doesn't count. There is no official rule book, of course, but I think most researchers would agree with the following.

The Research Needs to Be Reliable

Reliability is an important technical term in research methodology. A research process is reliable if you get similar results each time you repeat it. Research results can be considered reliable if repeated research efforts continually generate similar results. As communication scholars, we need to think about reliability because we understand that there are exceptions to even the strongest patterns of behavior, and we have to make sure that our results reflect the *rule* rather than the *exception.*

The Research Needs to Be Valid

The terms *valid* and *validity* mean that the research is capable of generating a meaningful understanding of reality or that the results of a research process reflect reality in some meaningful way. The primary criterion for judging research is reliability because if research is unreliable then questions of validity cannot even be raised. The secondary criterion is validity: If the research is reliable, then we have to consider whether it is valid. We have to consider whether it reflects reality in some meaningful way.

Think about studies attempting to make a connection between television content and violent behavior. Scholars conducting many of the early studies in this area had children watch television and then had them go into a room with a number of toys in it, one of which was a bobo doll. A bobo doll is an inflatable doll about the height of a small child. The doll has a rounded base full of sand and a large red clown nose. The toy is designed to be punched in the nose (which usually beeps or squeaks when struck) and then to swing back up so that it can be punched again. If the research is reliable (or, put another way, if there is a reliable connection between watching violent television content and acting violently), then children who watch violent television programs will consistently act more "violently" toward the bobo doll than will children who do not watch violent television programs. This is a relatively easy experiment and so can be conducted in a number of places, with different children of different ages watching different programs. If there is a consistent relationship between watching violent programs and punching bobo dolls, we can say the research findings are reliable. Only then does it make sense to ask if they are valid. Now we can ask: Is having children punch a toy that was designed to be punched by children really a measure of *violence?* On the other hand, if there were no consistent relationship found between watching television and punching the bobo doll, there would be no findings and so no need to ask if the findings were valid.

Obviously, we should *imagine* getting consistent results and then ask ourselves if these results would be valid. This saves a lot of time, effort, and money. The two concepts of reliability and validity will be discussed in greater detail throughout this text.

The Research Needs to Be Falsifiable

I mean this in a very weak sense. Research should be designed in such a way that it is possible for the researcher to find out that his or her ideas are wrong. Research is designed to do two things: provide support for ideas and rule out alternative explanations. Here's an example: A number of years ago I thought that people who used Apple computers were different in interesting and substantial ways from people who used DOS machines. Apple and DOS users, I believed, would have different values, different worldviews, and different attitudes toward science, the arts, and philosophy. Umberto Eco, the Italian semiotician, once said that Apple embodied a Protestant approach to the world and salvation, whereas DOS was more Catholic. I tested this idea by surveying undergraduate college students. My ideas were not supported. I modified the survey instrument and tried the following year, and again the year after that: No support. I was wrong. I could not support my ideas in any reliable manner.

If your ideas will be supported by *whatever* your research finds, then you are not really asking an empirical question. In this case, you are making a logical argument or are engaged in interpretation. In the past, the idea of falsification was married to a very rigid interpretation of research, one that was based in physical sciences such as chemistry and biology. This "hard science" model plays only a limited role in communication studies. Because of that, the claim made here is much softer than that made by the positivists, who were defending an idealized version of science. All that is meant here is that research cannot *presuppose* its conclusion and still be considered empirical research. This idea of falsifiability will be discussed in greater detail in Chapter 5.

The Research Needs to Be Useful

Research that serves no practical or intellectual purpose can still be valid. But one important way in which research is evaluated is by the extent to which it serves a useful purpose. The purpose can be purely intellectual: A theory is supported or refined, results of earlier research are replicated, or a new conceptualization of an old problem is tested. The purpose can be pragmatic, as it is in most private sector research: seeing how the market for a given product is changing, testing Web design effectiveness, or looking at communication flows within an organization. The purpose can be social change: examining the link between commercial culture and behavior, studying the impact of sexism on the education of children, or analyzing racial stereotypes in television drama.

We don't ask if the research is *true.* Instead, we ask about its reliability and validity. We want to know if the research actually leads us somewhere new and serves a critical purpose. Finally, we want to determine how useful the research is in some realm—intellectual, practical, or social.

AN OVERVIEW OF THE TEXT

In this book, we look at how the Rules of Looking are applied in four different areas of study: field research, experimentation, survey research, and content analysis.

Field research occurs "in the field." This means that to learn about the world, the researcher leaves the office or laboratory and goes out into the world of actual human interaction. A study of Hell's Angels, for example, should probably involve going on motorcycle rides, and that means one is engaging in fieldwork. Experimentation, on the other hand, generally takes place in a more controlled environment that is designed to exclude most of the complexity of real life. Survey research uses interviews conducted in person or by phone or via mailed questionnaires. Content analysis involves the examination of cultural products such as television programming, music lyrics, and the advice given in self-help books.

Each of these methodologies, or ways of getting information about the world, has both strong and weak points. Not one of them is the best. Which one we choose depends on the questions we are asking and the sorts of answers we are expecting. Partially, we choose methodologies on the basis of the way questions have been researched in the past, practical decisions, what best fits our personality, or how much time or money we have available. All of the methodologies presented in this book are good, and all of them have limitations. It is best to be able to use all of them.

This book is organized so that the technical aspects and terminology are discussed according to how they fit in each methodology. The questions we can ask in fieldwork, for example, are different from those we can ask in experimentation. But before we can begin to look at the different methodologies, it is necessary to discuss some of the basic concepts involved in research. Part I of the book provides the basic definitions and concepts needed to begin to understand research methods.

The ability to *conduct* research and the ability to *write* research reports are treated here as two sides of the same coin. Research methodology allows you to clarify your research means and goals and to justify your decisions. This is precisely what is needed for a research report: a clear statement of means and goals, justified on methodological grounds.

Part I of the book introduces terms and ideas that apply to all the methods covered in this text. It does this with the understanding that these terms and ideas work themselves out differently in fieldwork, experimentation, surveys, and content analysis. In both experiments and fieldwork, for example, you will need to think about sampling and variables, but these will be much more rigidly defined in an experiment than in fieldwork. The same is true of writing about research activities. Writing up the results of an experiment is not the same as writing up the results of field research.

METHOD AS WRITING, WRITING AS METHOD

The last chapter in Part I of this text is about writing research reports. There is a basic model for writing these reports, which is discussed. This model is then modified for each methodology discussed in Part II. Understanding the basic model is crucial, I believe, for understanding how the different methodologies are used. In the chapter on writing, research methodology is presented as a rhetorical strategy. Formalized research methods constitute a way of organizing and presenting a research project so that it is both clear and convincing. Research is a social activity. Researchers build on the work of others. Because of the social nature of research, a researcher must be able to let others know how and why the project was designed and conducted as it was. Clear interaction between members of the research communities and between the research communities and the larger society is critical. When we are made to think about *presenting* research, we are more careful because we are aware that our activity is, from its very inception, public.

In this book, the basic model for writing reports on empirical research is the academic journal model. This is the model that social scientists have borrowed, with modifications, from the physical sciences. However, various ways of presenting data in applied settings (business, public administration, consulting, etc.) are also discussed.

Though it is reasonable to distinguish between these two approaches to writing about research, it is important to understand that nonacademic styles are derived from the academic model and are quite self-consciously dependent on it. So although only a small percentage of those enrolled in undergraduate methods courses will ever publish in an academic journal, an understanding of how such an article is constructed is critical to anyone who creates or consumes research reports.

ACTIVITIES AND EXERCISES

1. The following news story was recently printed in the *San Francisco Chronicle.* It shows how data, by themselves, are not necessarily the result of research. What do you think of the controversy reported here? What would you like to know to resolve the debate, and how would you go about getting the information you needed? Read the story and look at the graphics that follow it; then answer the questions posed in this paragraph.

SIDEBAR 1.2 "Santa Clara County Angry Over Report: Officials Say State Crime Study Skewed" (Finz, 1998)

Although a new study says that Santa Clara County has seen the biggest increase in violent crime in California, officials say it's still one of the safest places to live in the state. The Legislative Analyst's Office found that violent crime in Santa Clara County had increased 17 percent from 1986 to 1996, while the state saw an average drop of 7.9 percent. Law enforcement officers argued yesterday that the study's numbers are misleading.

"The report is absurd and irresponsible," said District Attorney George Kennedy, who pointed to the county's significant decrease in homicides, rapes and robberies over the 10-year period. He says an 87.5 percent increase in reported aggravated assaults, which Kennedy and police attribute to a continuing crackdown on domestic violence, is skewing the numbers.

"The fact that more people are reporting domestic violence and the fact that we're making more arrests shows we're doing a good job, not a bad one," Kennedy said. "Other counties don't have as vigorous a program as we have."

Craig Cornett, director of criminal justice and state administration for the Legislative Analyst's Office, said there are many factors that can drive up the crime rate, including demographics, police practices and how comfortable residents are with reporting crimes. "There are so many things that can account for it, it's hard to tell," Cornett said.

Despite its 17 percent surge, Santa Clara County still has the second-lowest crime rate of the 15 largest counties in California, according to the study. San Mateo County ranked the safest, while San Francisco, Sacramento and Fresno counties had the most violence and property crimes.

"People shouldn't be freaking out," Cornett said. "Santa Clara has always been on the low side of crime." Acting San Jose Police Chief Walter Adkins says, "We are absolutely

(Continued)

SIDEBAR 1.2 Continued

convinced that domestic violence cases are increasing the numbers."

Until 10 years ago, the police rarely made arrests in domestic violence situations unless the victim was willing to testify, Adkins said. But laws and attitudes changed, he said. Soon, Santa Clara County had one of the most aggressive domestic violence programs in the state, Kennedy said.

SIDEBAR 1.3 "Santa Clara County Angry Over Report," Continued

Santa Clara County Crime Rates:
Reported Rates per 100,000 Population

Year	Homicide	Forcible Rape	Robbery	Aggravated Assault
1986	4.2	47.4	122.9	289.3
1996	2.9	33.2	108.3	402.8

Percent Change

SOURCE: Finz (1998).

2. The second story is reported in a news column in the *San Francisco Examiner.* This is also about the meaning of numbers and the perception of crime. Read the story, and answer the questions that follow it.

**SIDEBAR 1.4 "Back to School on Shootings"
(Morse, 1998, p. A2)**

More than a week after the latest school shooting in Oregon, the TV networks are still doing specials on guns and schools.

The supposed epidemic of school shootings has led legislators in several states to propose trying juveniles as adults, and even allowing them to be sentenced to death.

Gun control advocates have been thrown into a tizzy. Instead of going after guns sold out of automobile trunks in the inner city, they are forced politically to deal with the hunting guns used by kids in the rural shootings.

"We are legislating by sound bite instead of sound policy," says Vincent Schiraldi, in a pretty good sound bite.

He's used to having to make them. As director of the Center for Justice Policy Institute, this San Franciscan has had to go on CNN and add some needed facts to the uproar.

CNN's Greta Van Susteren didn't believe him when he said there is no epidemic of school shootings. But here are some statistics: In 1992, only 55 killings occurred in America's schools. In 1997 it was down to 25.

By contrast, 88 people were killed by lightning in 1997.

Schiraldi says he hates to see rural schools start spending money on metal detectors and security guards instead of books. "It's the functional equivalent of everyone buying lightning rods," he says.

Schiraldi says that in the last eight months, while the five highly publicized rural school shootings occurred, 933 juveniles were murdered in the inner city. He says people invariably ask if the kids were shot in the schools, and he responds, "No, but they're just as dead. Stop looking in the schools."

Consider that the Los Angeles County School System, with about 600,000 students, has not had a homicide since 1995.

(Continued)

SIDEBAR 1.4 Continued

Above all, consider that while the homicide rate in the U.S. dropped 20 percent between 1992 and 1996, the number of homicides reported on network news increased by 721 percent.

It's good for ratings, even if it may be bad for the psyches of children, voters and politicians. Fear sells. Kids are impressionable and may become copycats. Adults are impressionable and may pass bad laws.

Why do you think school shootings are getting such coverage? What do you think this says about the creation of social issues in this country? What are the symbolic issues involved here? Do you think social class or racism plays a role? What do you think is the politics of it? How would you go about supporting your ideas using empirical research?

2

DIVIDING UP THE WORLD:

Using Variables in the Social Sciences

In the social sciences, we are concerned with how things work *in general* rather than with why any particular person did any particular thing. We can say, for example, that men interrupt in conversations more frequently than women without suggesting that all men interrupt more than all women or that any particular man interrupts more than any particular woman. You may know women who interrupt continuously and men who never interrupt at all, but that doesn't negate the generalization that men interrupt more than women.

We arrive at these generalizations through the use of variables, or general categories. Thinking about the world in terms of variables is known as the variable-analytic approach. The opposite of the variable-analytic approach is the narrative approach, which is often seen in historical studies and in anthropological and sociological fieldwork. Other names for these two approaches are *nomothetic* (for *variable-analytic*) and *ideographic* (for *narrative*). The nomothetic approach will be discussed in the chapters on experiments and surveys (Chapters 7 and 8). The ideographic approach will be examined in the Chapter 6, on fieldwork, and, to a lesser extent, in Chapter 9, on content analysis.

SIDEBAR 2.1 Mnemonic Device

The way I remember these terms is that the variable analytic approach provides *no mo'* information than you need, whereas the ideographic approach provides *graphic* detail. Corny, but it works for me.

WHAT IS A VARIABLE?

Imagine that you have a large box divided into two compartments. The box is labeled "Conversational Styles," and one compartment is labeled "Interrupters," whereas the other is labeled "Noninterrupters." With this box in front of you, you sit in the campus cafeteria watching the people around you. You watch all the conversations that are taking place at the surrounding tables. You watch each conversational group for 3 minutes, and if, during that time, a man in the group interrupts someone else in the group, you drop a blue poker chip in the compartment labeled "Interrupters." If the man doesn't interrupt anyone, then you drop a blue chip in the compartment labeled "Noninterrupters." You do this for all the men, and, using red chips, you do the same for all the women. At the end of the day, you count the number of red and blue chips in each compartment. According to past research, there should be proportionately more blue than red chips in the "Interrupters" compartment and more red chips than blue chips in the "Noninterrupters" compartment (Figure 2.1).

This is a study using two variables: "Sex" and "Conversational Styles." Each variable has two attributes, or "values." "Sex" is divided into "male" and "female" (the blue and red chips). "Sex" is the variable; "male" and "female" are this variable's attributes. (Remember: Values and attributes are the same thing. Statistical software usually refers to attributes as *values*.) "Conversational Style" is divided into "interrupters" and "noninterrupters" (the two compartments). "Conversational Style" is the variable; "interrupters" and "noninterrupters" are its attributes.

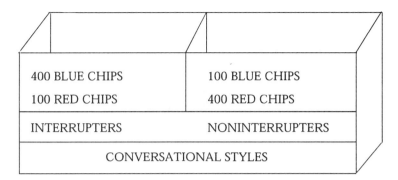

Figure 2.1. Picturing Variables

Dividing the world into variables is a way of simplifying it so that we can understand what is going on. There may be all sorts of reasons why Henry Johnson is interrupting Sally Brown on the morning when we are sitting in the cafeteria. He could be angry. She could be argumentative. He could have an upset stomach. She could be talking about something she knows nothing about, or they could be talking about something that threatens their core beliefs. The list could go on and on, and we, as researchers, do not care about any of it. What we want to know is whether men, in general, interrupt more than women.

SIDEBAR 2.2 Numbers and Proportions

The hypothesis is that men will interrupt more than women, but what if there are more women than men in the cafeteria? The argument would be that proportionately more men than women would interrupt. The important thing to note in Figure 2.1 is not that 400 men interrupted and only 100 women interrupted, but that four out of five men interrupted, whereas only one out of five women did so. Percentages usually give a more accurate picture than actual numbers.

SIDEBAR 2.3 Types of Studies

This study looks at variables that have two attributes. "Sex" has male/female, and "Conversational Styles" has interrupter/noninterrupter. Because we are trying to see how two attributes are related to two other attributes, we call this a two-by-two study design. If we wanted to see if time of day made a difference, we could divide the times we looked in the cafeteria into day and evening, which would give us a two-by-two-by-two design. If we thought, for some reason, that the day should be broken up into morning, afternoon, and evening, then we would have a two-by-two-by-three design.

The use of variables gets rid of information that is seen as irrelevant and allows us to obtain more usable information. James R. Beniger (1986) spoke of this variable-analytic approach, which he called *rationalization,* when he stated:

> Rationalization might be defined as the destruction or ignoring of information in order to facilitate its processing. . . . One example from within bureaucracy is the development of standardized paper forms. This might at first seem a contradiction, in that the proliferation of paperwork is usually associated with a growth in information to be processed, not with its reduction. Imagine how much more processing would be required, however, if each new case were recorded in an unstructured way, including every nuance and in full detail, rather than by checking boxes, filling blanks, or in some other way reducing the burdens of the bureaucratic system to only the limited range of formal, objective, and impersonal information. (pp. 15-16)

You can see from Beniger's account that the variable-analytic reduction of the rich complexity of life is a way of ignoring

SIDEBAR 2.4 Demographic Variables

Demographic variables are important and commonly used because they can place people into broad categories. Demographic variables concern place of birth, race or ethnicity, sex, age, social status or class, religious affiliation, educational level, occupation, place of residence, and so on.

information in order to obtain information. In the variable-analytic tradition, you always have to weigh what you gain against what you lose.

DESCRIPTIONS AND EXPLANATIONS

The way we use variables depends on what kind of research methods we are using and the theories and hypotheses we have. In the conversational styles example, for instance, we can say that sex *explains* conversational styles because if we know what sex someone is, we can make informed guesses about their tendency to interrupt. Or we can say that sex differences in conversational styles *describe* a pattern of interaction that is in need of explanation. This is an important distinction and will be repeated throughout this book: What something means and which method you use are dependent on what you want to do and the sorts of explanations you are interested in testing. Methods and data are things you use.

You could say, for example, that a person's conversational style is *explained* by his or her sex: Men interrupt, women do not. In newspapers, daytime talk shows, and casual conversation, we hear this sort of "explanation" all the time: "He talks that way because he's a man"; "He didn't score well on the SAT exam because he's black"; "She acts that way because she's Italian." Unless, however, we want to attribute a great deal of power to testosterone or to skin color or to one's ancestors' place of birth, many times these sorts of *demographic* variables do not help a great deal in trying to understand what is going on. Frequently, demographic variables are *symbols* of something else, such as social status, education, accepted sex roles, religious beliefs, or generational differences. You should keep this in mind whenever "whites" are compared to "nonwhites" or men to women.

We know that the conversational styles are based in something other than the presence or absence of certain sex organs because not all the men in the cafeteria study were interrupters and not all the women were noninterrupters. So it can't be a purely biological relationship: It isn't like the relationship between being a female and getting pregnant. Given this, what other *variables* could you use to explain the differences we found?

WHAT DO YOU THINK?

The variables that you would use to explain sex differences are those that would make the most sense to you. What makes sense to you is based on your personality and your experiences as well as your cultural and educational backgrounds. The more you delve into a topic, the more your ideas will be shaped by the theories and research of fellow scholars. The origin of the ideas is not critical here because we are going to *test* them. Research methodologies, in a way, stand between what "makes sense to us" and the conclusions we can legitimately accept.

If you think of being a man or a woman as primarily a *biological* condition, then you might want to ask the people in the cafeteria for blood samples and check their hormone levels. The variables that you might use to account for differences in conversational styles would be "Testosterone Levels" or "Estrogen Levels" because these are related to sexual identity. You could divide these variables into low, medium, and high levels of testosterone or estrogen to see if the men who interrupted had higher levels than the men who didn't. (Exactly how these attributes of high, medium, and low are determined will be discussed in Chapter 8, on surveys.)

Another way of getting at the biological question would be to use culture as a variable and see if people from different cultures showed similar patterns. If the difference was really based in biology, then Americans, Germans, Australian Aborigines, Japanese, and Tibetans would all show patterns of conversational style similar to those found in the cafeteria. A comparison of the interruption patterns of people from different cultures would show whether men, regardless of culture, tend to interrupt and whether women, regardless of culture, do not.

If you think about sex in more sociological terms, then the differences you observed in the cafeteria might have to do with power differences between men and women. Your theory might be that men interrupt to assert power; women do not interrupt because they are socially subordinate. If this was the way you wanted to look at gender differences in conversational style, then you could add social class as a variable on the assumption that socially dominant men and women interrupt, whereas socially subordinate men and women do not. Or you could look at interactions between superiors and subordinates at work to see if superiors, regardless of whether they are men or women, tended to be interrupters. These different uses of variables are summarized in Table 2.1.

You can see that variables are categories that have attributes. These categories are things that we create to make sense of the world. There are different kinds of variables that serve different purposes in research. These different kinds of variables will be discussed as we work through the different types of research presented in this text.

TYPES OF VARIABLES

All of the examples of variables discussed above had either two or three attributes, but variables can have an infinite number of

Table 2.1 Descriptive and Explanatory Questions

Do men and women have different patterns of turn taking in conversation?

Variables	Attributes
Sex	Male, female
Conversational Styles	Interrupters, noninterrupters

Why do men and women have different patterns of turn taking in conversation?

Biological Model	
Variables	Attributes
Hormone Levels	High, medium, low
Culture	French, Jamaican, American, Mexican, Chinese, etc.

Sociological Model	
Variables	Attributes
Social Class	High, medium, low
Social Status	Professional, managerial, blue collar, pink collar

Psychological Model	
Variables	Attributes
Self-Esteem	High, medium, low

attributes. "Age," for example, can be a variable, and aging, as we all know, is something that happens second by second from the moment of birth until the moment of death. In general, however, we count our age by years rather than seconds, so "Age" is a variable that could quite easily have 80 or 90 attributes: one for each year a person could claim.

Let's imagine that you think of age as a variable that could help explain the different ways students interact in class. The attributes could include all possible ages, or these possible ages could be "bundled" into more manageable categories. How you handle

Table 2.2 Variable and Attributes

Variable = Age	
Attribute A:	17, 18, 19, 20, 21, 22, 23, 24, 25, etc.
Attribute B:	17-20, 21-25, 26-30, 31-35, etc.
Attribute C:	traditional students (25 or younger), nontraditional students (26 or older)

the data depends on the kinds of questions you are asking and how you expect to analyze the data (Table 2.2).

How you decide to organize your attributes is up to you. All you have to do is be able to justify your decisions in terms of the questions you are asking. Remember: Research methodology is designed to help you answer questions, not to hinder your research or creativity.

Because variables are simply categories that we make up in order to make sense of the world, there is virtually no limit to the number of variables we could use. It may sound a bit odd, but variables do not exist in the physical world. Variables are ways we catalogue the world, so they exist only in the realm of consciousness. We can use variables to organize all different aspects of life, but, in general, variables fall into a limited number of categories: demographics, behavior, attitudes and beliefs, things, and events (Table 2.3).

Variables are ways that we divide the world rather than ways the world is divided. This can be easily demonstrated by looking at how people in different cultures or at different times conceptualize reality. For example, it is obvious that we are born either male or female, and in our culture we see this as a very important distinction. Sex tends to be one of our most popular variables. One of the ways we know this is important is that have words that mark the distinction: Some children are boys, and some children are girls. This distinction between boys and girls, however, was not always considered significant. The word *girl* used to mean

Table 2.3 Variable Types

Type	Examples
Demographic	Age, income, religion, years of education, sex, etc.
Behavior	Votes, smokes, exercises, treats people differently based on religion, etc.
Attitudes	Bigoted, civic-minded, honest, frightened, optimistic, etc.
Beliefs	Can get AIDS from toilet seats, democrats are communists, republicans are bigots, women are emotional, men are violent, etc.
Things	Types of material goods, neighborhoods, housing, etc.
Events	Violent acts, polite gestures, riots, initiation rites, etc.

any small child, regardless of sex. Although there was no word for female children, there was a word for male children. So at least as late as the 15th century, children were divided into "boys" and "children-in-general." There was no word for female children because they were not important enough to be noticed. (One should not assume from this that boys were liked and that other kinds of children were not liked. The word *boy* is derived from the word for *slave,* so maybe there were two kinds of children: those who could labor and those who could not.)

This example should show you that the differences that variables draw attention to must indicate actual differences in the world, but *which* differences we consider important depends to a great extent on our creativity, interests, values, intellectual history, social position, culture, language, and era. We create the world in the process of understanding it.

RULES ABOUT ATTRIBUTES

A variable is a collection of attributes. That much you already know. The attributes of a variable need to have two qualities: they must be *mutually exclusive,* and they must be *exhaustive.*

A variable's attributes are mutually exclusive if it is not possible for whatever is being examined to have two attributes. Put another way, any given case can only have one attribute. Think of sex: If we ignore hermaphrodites and transsexuals, this is a variable that has two mutually exclusive attributes. If a person is a male, then that person cannot be a female, and if a person is a female, then that person cannot be a male. Compare the variable "Sex" to the variable "Sexual Orientation," and it is easy to see that the common (and usually workable) division into hetero- and homosexual lacks mutual exclusivity. If *heterosexual* means "sexually attracted to members of the opposite sex" and *homosexual* means "sexually attracted to members of the same sex," then what would we do with people who are bisexual? Bisexuals could claim both attributes, and that means the two attributes are not mutually exclusive.

Think of variables as multiple-choice questions. A multiple-choice question in which more than one answer is possible is a bad question.

Another problem with variables occurs when the attributes are not exhaustive. That is like having a multiple-choice question in which none of the answers is correct.

A variable is exhaustive if its attributes cover all possible cases. Imagine the variable "Marital Status." There are two basic attributes for marital status: unmarried and married. This dichotomy is exhaustive in that it covers all adults. Sometimes these two attributes will provide all the information that one needs to know. "Marital Status" is a variable on tax forms, for example, and all that the IRS wants to know is whether you are married or unmarried. If we wanted to look at the connection (if any) between marital status and happiness, we might find this two-attribute variable too limiting. If we "unpacked" these attributes, we could separate people into categories for all the different ways a person can be married or unmarried. A married person could be a newlywed, a person who has been married twice or three times or more, a person who is married but separated, a person waiting for the final divorce decree, or a person who has been married to the same person for 25 years. Unmarried people include widows, never-marrieds, divorcées, and people engaged to be married for the fifth time.

Imagine that we have "Ethnicity" as a variable and we ask people to check off the ethnicity with which they identify. We can give the following list:

- African American
- European American
- Asian American
- American Indian
- Hispanic American

This list looks complete. We know it ignores a great deal, but that is not necessarily a problem. All European origins are considered the same, for example, in that Swedes are lumped with Italians and Spaniards. The same is true for Asians, Africans, Hispanics, and American Indians, as if there were no important differences between, say, being Chinese and being Pakistani. But it meets the *exhaustiveness* criterion—or does it? In the United States, as in other multicultural societies, people of one background can marry people of another background, and the result will be people who cannot find a place on this list. Which box would you check if one of your parents was of Germanic heritage and the other of American Indian heritage? This list is not exhaustive. If you can easily imagine a person who cannot find a place on your list, then the list is not exhaustive.

Life is complicated, and variables reduce the complexity—but don't let them reduce it to the point where they lose all validity. Variables are used to create arguments, and the easiest way to dismiss an argument is to attack the variables used. Because variables form the skeleton on which an empirical argument hangs, the next chapter will look at the creation of variables. It will be about how variables are operationalized so that they can be used in research.

SIDEBAR 2.5 Vocabulary

Attribute	Demographic	Ideographic	Narrative	Nomothetic
Unit of analysis	Values	Variable	Variable-analytic	

SUMMARY

1. A variable is a category that has attributes. *Example:* "Sex" is a variable that has the attributes male and female. *Example:* "Testosterone Levels" is a variable with the attributes high, medium, and low.
2. Variables are ways of simplifying the world in order to understand general patterns.
3. Variables are used both to describe and to explain things.
4. There are different kinds of variable attributes, and there is no set number of attributes per variable.

ACTIVITIES AND EXERCISES

1. If "Liberal," "Moderate," and "Conservative" are the *attributes,* then what is the *variable?*
2. Some people have argued for "using shame to control out-of-wedlock births among teenagers." The two variables in this statement are "shame" and "out-of-wedlock births." What is being used to explain what? In a paragraph, write what you think the theory is that relates these two variables.
3. On your campus, what are the attributes of the variable "Course Grade"?
4. What are the different kinds of variables mentioned in the text? Give an example of each kind of variable. (For example, "Age" is an example of a demographic variable.)

5. In Table 2.1, "culture" is included in the "Biological Model."
Why?

6. Consider the following abstract, and answer Questions A
through C on a separate sheet of paper.

This research project examined questions concerning the effectiveness of female managers using stereotypically masculine or feminine communication management styles. Nurses
from three hospitals were surveyed on the perceptions of the
communication management style of their superiors and answered self-report questions about their morale and job satisfaction. Employees of female managers who were perceived
as managing in a stereotypically feminine style reported significantly greater morale and job satisfaction than did employees whose female managers were perceived as managing in
a stereotypically masculine style. Implications are discussed.
(Camden & Kennedy, 1986, p. 551)

A. What are the three variables in this study?
B. What is the relationship between the variables? (Which vari-
able(s) is (are) *being explained,* and which variable(s) is (are) *being used as explanations?*
C. Why do you think Camden and Kennedy, the authors, tell us
that the measures of morale and job satisfaction are self-report
variables?

3

OPERATIONALIZATION:

Just Exactly What Do You Mean by That?

The key to good research is clarity. The problem with many research projects is that it is not really clear what is meant by the variables that are used. Obviously, this is not a serious problem with variables like "Sex," but what if you are trying to measure romantic intensity, a good education, attractiveness, a successful marriage, or a biased news report? Suddenly, something that seems quite clear in casual conversation becomes incredibly complex.

A good example of this is television violence. It would seem reasonably clear what violence means until one actually goes looking for it in prime time television. Remember the example above in which we had a box with compartments labeled "Interrupters" and "Noninterrupters." Now we need a box with two compartments labeled "Violent" and "Nonviolent." We take this box and sit in front of the television set watching prime time evening programming, and we have to decide whether it is violent or not. We'll go into this sort of problem in greater detail in Chapter 9 on content analysis, but just imagine the sort of cases you'd have to consider:

- A gangster is seen firing a gun, and a man is later found dead.
- A mother lashes out with a rolling pin and knocks unconscious a man who is trying to molest her daughter.
- A police officer sitting on the steps of a house tells us that someone inside has been horribly murdered.
- Roger Rabbit hits himself in the head with a hammer.
- A gunshot is heard, and a man falls, dead, to the floor without any cry of pain or indication of a wound.
- A beginning driver gets a blowout, loses control of her car, and runs over a small child.
- A villain slaps a woman cashier during a robbery.
- A police officer shoots and kills an armed robber who shot at her.

To consider any of these as instances of television violence, we would have to have a very clear *definition* of violence and then a very clear *operationalization* of violence. The *definition* (also known as the *conceptualization*) tells us what sort of thing to look for. The *operationalization* spells out the criteria for saying that something is, or is not, an "act of violence."

For example, if we *define* violence as any action that results in, or is intended to result in, injury to another person, then we have to decide if Roger Rabbit is a "person." We would then have to *operationalize* "person" as either "any character capable of playing a role in a story" (which would include animated rabbits) or "any actual human being depicted" (which excludes both animated rabbits and animated humans such as GI Joe and Elmer Fudd).

It is amazing how difficult it is to operationalize even obvious things such as television violence. Should the mother protecting her daughter, the driver with the blowout, and the police officer be lumped in the same category as the gangster and the cashier-slapping villain? And, because we're talking about violence in a visual medium, do we have to *see* the "actions resulting in injury" for them to count? The policeman sitting on the steps tells us about the body inside, indicating that a murder has occurred, but

SIDEBAR 3.1 Operationalizing "Road Rage"

The following is an excerpt from Michael Fumento's "'Road Rage' Versus Reality" (1998). In the excerpt, Fumento primarily questions the way road rage is defined and operationalized. Read these remarks, and ask yourself how you would define and operationalize road rage.

Still, aggressive driving does cause some accidents. At Petri's subcommittee hearings Martinez claimed that "one third of these crashes and about two thirds of the resulting fatalities can be attributed to behavior associated with aggressive driving." The media accepted this claim without question: "TEMPER CITED AS CAUSE OF 28,000 ROAD DEATHS A YEAR" (the *New York Times*); "TWO-THIRDS OF ALL AUTO DEATHS BLAMED ON STRESSED-OUT, AGGRESSIVE DRIVERS" (the *San Francisco Examiner*); "SEETHING MOTORISTS MAKE CARS WEAPONS" (the *Albany Times Union*). But was there any truth to the figure of 28,000?

Liz Neblett, a spokeswoman for the NHTSA, responded quite candidly. "We don't have hard numbers," she said, "but aggressive driving is almost everything. It includes weaving in and out of traffic, driving too closely, flashing your lights—all kinds of stuff. Drinking, speeding, almost everything you can think of, can be boiled down to aggressive driving behaviors." With such a broad definition, Martinez could conceivably label virtually every accident as the result of aggressive driving.

Arnold Nerenberg, a clinical psychologist in Whittier, California . . . claims that more than half of drivers have "road-rage disorder." Sometimes he describes this as "basically a maladaptive reaction to an identifiable psychosocial stressor that interferes with social functioning." When he wants to be understood, he calls it "one driver expressing anger at another driver . . . at least twice a year."

(Continued)

Nerenberg has his own road-rage statistics. During a CNN interview he said, "Fifty-three percent of our population has a road-rage disorder," and 1.78 billion "episodes" occur each year. "That's based on the fact that on average drivers manifest road rage twenty-seven times a year, and we have about a hundred and twenty-five million cars on the road." Nerenberg considers road rage a "mental disorder and a social disease," and proposes that it be included in the *Diagnostic and Statistical Manual of Mental Disorders* of the American Psychiatric Association. (p. 16)

we see nothing. We see the gangster fire his gun, but do not see the bullet hit anyone. We see the man clutch his chest and crumple silently to the floor, but we see no causal action. Are these instances of *television violence?* If the situations listed above occurred in one evening's programming, would it be informative or misleading to say that there were eight acts of violence on television that night?

And then there are smaller but equally difficult problems. What if the gangster shoots the person twice? Is that one act of violence or two? What if only seconds lapse between the two shots? What if minutes go by? Days? Years? At what point does it become two distinct actions? All this has to be decided. It has to be *operationalized.*

But the problem of operationalization does not just occur in content analysis. It occurs in all research. Even the fictional study about interrupters and noninterrupters described in Chapter 2 requires some operationalization: If we are looking to see whether people interrupt, we have to know what interrupting looks like. A person can interrupt with an expression or a gesture as well as with words—should these count? What would constitute an interrupting gesture or expression? And what about all that conversational maintenance we do while listening—all the nods, and "hmmms," "yeses," and "uh huhs"? How do we objectively distinguish these sounds—known as "backchannels"—from interruptions? Obviously, noninterrupters are not passive, silent listeners: They can be passionately and enthusiastically involved in a conversation.

Although the research tradition on conversational interruptions follows the outline presented in the chapter on variables, some researchers have been skeptical. One of these researchers, Kathryn Dindia (1987), looked at the research on sex differences in interruptions because she believed that earlier studies had analyzed the data incorrectly. To demonstrate her point, she conducted new research using the same operationalizations used in the earlier research. She stated, "Interruptions were operationally defined as occurring when the listener began to speak at a point that was not a possible completion point for the speaker's utterance. . . . Backchannels were not included as interruptions."

Dindia defined five different types of interruptions, based on their content: clarification, agreement, disagreement, tangentialization, and subject change. Each one of these is operationalized.

THE POINT OF OPERATIONALIZATION

We frequently speak about liberals and conservatives, but how would we operationalize either of these concepts? What about other common terms like *middle class, educated, attractive, oppression,* or *polite?* To talk about these things in an objective and reliable manner, we must be very clear about what we mean. We have to be able to spell out in some detail exactly how we will "know it when we see it."

The point of operationalizing a term or a concept is to

- State clearly exactly what we mean by the term, in the context in which it is being researched
- State clearly what it means for something to be included or excluded from a category

SIDEBAR 3.2 Let's Get Critical: Ideas and Data

The following is an excerpt from a newspaper article titled "When It Comes to Men's Mugs, Softer Is Sexier: Women Attracted to Feminine Faces" (1998, p. A3):

Given a choice between a dewy-looking Leonardo DiCaprio type and a rugged Sean Connery sort of guy, women may be naturally attracted to the man with the more feminine face, researchers say.

. . . In separate experiments in Scotland and Japan, researchers created a composite "average" face for a man and a woman from about 30 digital photos. The faces were then altered at key points, including the eyes, lips, nose, and eyebrows, to make them more feminine or masculine.

Ninety-two volunteers—college students and staff members, ages 18 to 44, including 44 women—were asked to rate the faces according to such factors as warmth, emotionality, honesty, intelligence and dominance.

Both men and women preferred a more feminine face.

Questions

Why do they say "naturally" attracted? What is the evidence for this? Why is this an important or interesting thing to say?

How many respondents were involved? Two experiments—one in Japan and one in Scotland—means that the 92 volunteers were divided between different experiments. This means we can assume that about 22 women were used to represent Scottish women (who, in turn, represent European women). How many of these 22 women preferred DiCaprio over Connery? And by what margin? We have no idea. Is this enough to support a claim about *natural* preferences?

And where does this idea of preference come from? The claim is that "both men and women preferred a more

(Continued)

SIDEBAR 3.2 Continued

feminine face," but the description of the research said that the photos were judged on "such factors as warmth, emotionality, honesty, intelligence and dominance." If I say that DiCaprio looks warmer, more emotional, more honest, and less dominating than Connery, does that mean I *prefer* him or find him more attractive? (You'll notice I left out "intelligent." I just couldn't bring myself to say that DiCaprio looks more intelligent than Connery.) Isn't Connery attractive precisely because he looks like a rogue—a man who may lie to you, who may be a bit ruthless and domineering, who may not tell you his innermost feelings, and who may not exude warmth? Who defined *attractive* here, and what was the basis for the definition? We should also ask if *softer* means the same as *feminine*.

We could conclude from this research report that editors prefer soft, cute stories over news with a harder edge—but then, I think we would need some more data for that.

- Make it possible for another researcher to replicate (repeat) or expand on our study

It is important to understand that definitions and operationalizations, though crucial for good empirical research, are not themselves empirical research activities. Defining or operationalizing a concept is a creative intellectual activity governed, to use the expression in the introductory chapter, by the Rules of Thinking rather than the Rules of Looking. Because of this, we can reject a research project by rejecting the definitions and operationalizations on which it was based.

Recently, for example, I had a student who operationalized the quality of being "Christian" in such narrow terms that most people who consider themselves Christians were excluded. The operationalization was clear enough to conduct research on whether a sermon contained "the" Christian message, but the research had to be rejected because the definition and operationalization of *Christian* was without any social, intellectual, or historical basis. Again, we must go back to the ideas expressed in the opening chapter: The purpose of adhering to research methods guidelines is to design a research program that has the potential (a) to produce conclusions that run counter to your expectations and beliefs and (b) to convince people who do not agree with your positions. If you can reach your conclusions purely through logical analysis, then you are not engaged in empirical research and do not need to follow research methods.

Consider, for example, all the talk about sex on television. Because we know that commercial television does not present graphic depictions of sexual intercourse, let us define "sex on television" as "the presentation of individuals, male or female, as primarily sexual beings whose principal purpose is to arouse the sexual interest of the consumers." That may need some fine-tuning, but it is at least one of the major ways it is possible to talk about sex on television. Now, given this definition, we sit down in front of the television set to ascertain the extent to which television portrayals are sexual. Separate operationalizations would probably have to be drawn for male and female characters, but let us imagine that we operationalize a female character whose "principal purpose is to arouse the sexual interest of the consumers" as any female character whose skirt is above the knee.[1] (A student in this course once operationalized it this way.)

This is certainly clear and usable—but is it meaningful? It will mean that virtually all women on television are presented as sex objects, including Barbara Walters. This operationalization sounds more like an ideological than an empirical position. A great many open-minded, honest, nonsexist, nondegenerate Americans would find this operationalization far too broad.

We could separate out female characters as being primarily sexual arousers if they wear "sexy clothes." But though we all may know sexy clothes when we see them, they are very difficult to operationalize. In one class in which students looked at ads, one group of women described the young women in a set of ads as being "cute" and "perky," whereas another group described

SIDEBAR 3.3 Thinking Critically: From a Study of Lawns

If we assign the word grass to refer to plants with thin, green spike leaves that make up a good lawns then the dialectic symbolically transforms such grasses, but not all, e.g., "crabgrass," . . . into lawns. All "broadleafed" plants like dandelions, on the other hand, are then transformed into weeds. (Weigery, 1994, p. 82)

Weigery was studying the social status of front lawns—the meaning of those useless, labor-intensive patches of cultivated grass that are the distinguishing feature of suburban life—and understood that even things as prosaic as grass and weeds need to be defined. He saw that lawns indicate a great deal about our worldviews and about the way we divide up reality. (Flowers sprouting in my lawn are weeds, as is grass growing in my flower beds: It's all relative—and somewhat moralistic.)

The importance of this passage is that, quite frequently in variable-analytic research, by defining and operationalizing one concept we implicitly define and operationalize others. When we define what is normal, good, expected, preferred, or natural, we are automatically also defining what is abnormal, bad, unexpected, disliked, and unnatural. This may be inconsequential in terms of grass and weeds, but it has significant implications if the context is education, relationships, culture, mental and physical health, or politics.

them as being "sluts." Some things are not as obvious as they seem.

In a critique of scientific research into human life, Neil Postman (1993) argued that

in the ranking of intelligence, we therefore assume that intelligence is not only a thing, but a single thing, located in the brain, and accessible to the assignment of a number. It is as if "beauty" were determined to adhere in the size of a woman's breasts. All we would have to do is measure breasts and rank each woman accordingly, and we would have an "objective" measure of "beauty." (p. 41)

Though Postman is being sarcastic, we know that there are people—maybe all of us in varying degrees—who "operationalize" beauty by measuring body parts, both male and female. Postman's example clearly illustrates the trade-off between reliability and validity. Reducing either beauty or intelligence to a number requires doing tremendous violence to the concepts as they are traditionally used. And the danger, exemplified by beauty contests and IQ tests, is that this conceptual narrowmindedness will leak out of the laboratory and into the real world, where such measures will be treated as valid.

It may help here to look at a few studies in which operationalizations have played a key role.

An Example

Academic journal articles frequently have "abstracts" or summaries at the beginning of the first page. To understand how operationalization works, we will look at a few of these abstracts. The first example is from an article entitled "Cultural Differences in the Retelling of Television Fiction" by Tamar Liebes (1988):

Within the broader study of how viewers from different cultures interpret American television texts, this article examines differences in viewer's retellings of an episode of *Dallas*. In settings designed to simulate normal viewing circumstances, small homogenous groups from five distinct cultural backgrounds watched an episode and then were asked how they would retell the story to someone who had not seen the show. The coding of the group retellings reveals correlations between ethnicity and choice of narrative form—classified as "linear,"

> **SIDEBAR 3.4 Excerpt from Bob Secter's "The 'Science' of Made-to-Order Statistics: Slyly Comparing Apples and Oranges Often Rationalized as Serving a Higher Cause" (1995, p. A2)**
>
> The sky is falling. If you have any doubts, consider this:
>
> In a nationwide survey of 2,000 youngsters aged 10 to 16 published by the American Academy of Pediatrics and widely reported by the news media, one out of four said they had been sexually or physically abused in the previous year.
>
> Not just in their lifetime. In a single year!
>
> If you do the math, assault seems as common an adolescent affliction as acne—some six million American kids annually being stomped, whomped on or otherwise subjected to unspeakable horrors.
>
> Except to reach these shocking numbers, researchers had to stretch the definition of abuse beyond rape, robbery, molestation, criminal assault and the like to include such activities as being shoved by your brother or getting into a schoolyard fight.
>
> Under those terms, the most startling part of the study is that it managed to find kids who said they hadn't been victimized.

"segmented," or "thematic"—which, in turn, reflect viewers' perceptions of the program and their own worlds. (p. 277)

Because you may be unfamiliar with the journal version of academic English, I'll translate some of this. Saying "American television texts" is the same as saying "American television shows" except that it sounds more European and respectable. Mass media scholars refer to the content of the mass media as "text." When Liebes refers to the "coding" of the group retellings, she means that she has reduced their "narratives" (what the people actually said) to variables. The variable she has reduced them to is "narrative form," which she tells us has three attributes: linear form, segmented form, and thematic form.

These are the three attributes that need to be operationalized. Sometimes students think that everything has to be operationalized—"television," *Dallas*, "episode," and so on—but really all you have to operationalize are the attributes you are trying to explain or the attributes you are using as an explanation. In this case, Liebes is using a demographic variable (native cultures of the subjects) to explain differences in narrative form. This demographic variable is not conceptually difficult, so Liebes does not spend too much time operationalizing it. She states:

> Groups were chosen from four widely different subcultures in Israel (Arabs, Moroccan Jews, new immigrants from Russia, second generation Israelis living in a kibbutz) and from second generation Americans living in Los Angeles. Approximately 10 groups were assembled within each community, each group consisting of three couples of like ethnicity. Age, education, and regular viewing of the program were essentially homogenous [i.e., the same] for all participants. (p. 278)

By telling us this, we now know what she means by the reference in the abstract to "five distinct cultural backgrounds." That is the purpose of operationalizing a variable. Liebes had the idea that people from different cultures would understand a story told on American television in different ways. We ask, "Well, what do you mean by different cultures?" and she tells us. We ask, "What do you mean by 'group'?" And she tells us: three couples of like ethnicity. We say, "Okay, but societies are complex things, and ethnic identity is only one of many identities a person can have. What about age and education? How do you distinguish between those who watch this program all the time and people who have never seen it before?" She tells us.

Now it is clear what Liebes is talking about, and we can go on to ask the more important question: "What do you mean by understanding and telling stories in different ways?" Liebes must now tell us what she means by linear, segmented, and thematic forms. This, of course, is more complicated than simply identifying what is meant by different cultures. Because of its complexity, Liebes's explanation will not be repeated in full. Instead, I will just reproduce a part of what she says about the segmented form: "[A] segmented, or indexical, analysis focuses on the characters, their motivation, and their interrelations. Thus a segmented retelling might identify a character and recount his or her interactions with different situations or with other characters in no particular sequence" (p. 281).

So the differences are that one can retell the story in the order presented (linear), can jump around in the story to explain a character (segmented), or can look for meaning (thematic). In her discussion of what people said, Liebes provides examples of the different ways the people in different groups talked about the episode.

Now when we read Liebes's conclusion we will know exactly what it is based on. This does not mean that we must accept it as true or accurate. It means that Liebes has provided us with a clear picture of what she did and what she means by key concepts. We can now look, if we are so inclined, at her research and criticize it on rational grounds, attacking either her methodology or her conceptualization.

Note that this is an example of operationalization in the context of research that blends *narrative* research and *nomothetic* research. A great deal of content analysis research blends these two approaches because content analysis frequently involves both interpretation and counting. Though operationalization is frequently associated with purely quantitative research, this example shows that it is always crucial that the reader know exactly what you are talking about.

A Second Example

James Beniger (1983) wrote an article entitled "Does Television Enhance the Shared Symbolic Environment? Trends in Labeling of Editorial Cartoons, 1948-1980." The abstract reads:

The diffusion of television may increase the proportion of a population that recognizes various public figures and more abstract cultural symbols. This hypothesis is tested with time series of the labeling used in 1,154 editorial cartoons of five leading U.S. metropolitan newspapers. The sample includes at least a hundred cartoons published in each of the nine presidential election years, 1948-1980. Both the proportion of actual persons labeled and the mean [i.e., average] number of labeled cartoons decreased by one-half to two-thirds over the period. . . . Several explanations other than the hypothesized increase in the shared symbolic environment are considered and rejected. Temporal correlation and other indirect inference suggest that television is at least a partial cause of the change. Television's influence on shared images is also noted by the cartoonists themselves. The findings suggest that television may increase the likelihood that cultural symbols can be used to direct a nation's attention, to manipulate public attention, and to mobilize behavior. (p. 103)

The *hypothesis* is the idea that a researcher is testing. In this case, it is clearly stated: Beniger believes that one of the things television has done is increase our shared symbolic environment. The "shared symbolic environment" is the totality of common understandings, shared beliefs and values, and generally understood facts within a society. Though this idea makes sense on the face of it (i.e., it has what is known as *face validity*), it is a very difficult thing to determine in any objective manner. Anyone trying to research an idea as large and inclusive as a shared symbolic environment must find some way of simplifying it so that it can be tested.

What makes Beniger's article really creative is not his ideas about television and shared environments but his way of operationalizing the idea of shared environments in such a way that it can be looked at empirically. When there is not a generally shared symbolic environment, the use of symbols is not very effective. Editorial cartoons are dependent on symbols because

SIDEBAR 3.5 Operationalization in Practice

Why is a mixed-race child, born in the United States of one white and one black parent, considered black? It makes as much sense genetically to call the child white. According to F. James Davis, the child is likely more than 50 percent white since the average American black has between 15 and 20 percent white ancestry. Further, why is such a classification accepted by both blacks and whites? (Wood, 1993, p. 243)

What is in question here is the *operationalization* of race. In some countries, people with one black and one white parent are called mulattos. In the United States, however, race has been *defined* in such a way that it is possible to inherit only one. Race has been *operationalized* in terms of what Davis called the "one-drop" rule. The one-drop rule states that one black ancestor negates all white ancestors.

This operationalization can be evaluated in terms of its usefulness, its genetic assumptions, its ideological or historical development, or its legal or social consequences. Race is one of the many interesting variables used by social scientists and by ordinary people. Like a great many of these interesting variables, the idea of race or ethnicity makes surface sense but is tricky to operationalize.

The simplicity of the one-drop rule increases the *reliability* of the concept of race, but what about its *validity?* You may think that it makes sense to call a person with one black and three white grandparents a black person. Does it make the same sense if it is one black and three American Indian grandparents? What about one Asian and three white grandparents? How would you operationalize race?

they have to pack so much meaning into such a very small space: the U.S. economy in one picture with a five-word caption. Russia (and later the USSR) becomes the Russian bear, the United States is Uncle Sam, and the U.S. war effort is symbolized by GI Joe. If these symbols aren't understood, then they have to be labeled. The reduction in the number of symbols labeled and in the number of cartoons in which labels appear, Beniger reasoned, would indicate an increase in shared symbol use. Thus, a huge idea like the "shared symbolic environment" becomes operationalized as the proportion of labels in editorial cartoons. And this operationalization makes a vague, intellectual cocktail party idea into a question that can be researched.

SUMMARY

To operationalize an idea is to state it in terms that can be researched empirically. It is to state it so clearly that a person reading the article can use the same operationalization in a new research project—which is, you remember, what Dindia did in contesting the idea that men interrupt more than women.

Much of the creativity in social science research lies in finding new ways of operationalizing intellectual ideas that enable us to remove them from the realm of purely logical debate. The debate over television violence, for example, is carried on as a purely intellectual debate—a matter of logic and values—with very little regard for what "television violence" means. To clearly state, in measurable terms (and if you can use the terms *more* or *less* in connection with a concept, then the assumption is that the concept is measurable) what "violence on television" or "sex on television" means is to present your ideas in such a way that they can actually be tested. This may be intellectually respectable (at least in some circles), but it is death in a political debate.

OPERATIONALIZATION IN PRACTICE

Although the federal government is usually associated with incompetence, it is amazingly good at some things. One of the things it is really good at is research and the dissemination of information (at least of information that is not considered secret) on Web pages. The following is from a document entitled *How the Government Measures Unemployment*, produced by the U.S. Bureau of Labor Statistics (1995). This document explains clearly what is meant by the term *unemployed.* The following excerpt is an excellent example of operationalization.

What Are the Basic Concepts of Employment and Unemployment?

The basic concepts involved in identifying the employed and unemployed are quite simple:

- People with jobs are employed.
- People who are jobless, looking for jobs, and available for work are unemployed.
- People who are neither employed nor unemployed are not in the labor force.

The survey is designed so that each person age 16 and over who is not in an institution such as a prison or mental hospital or on active duty in the Armed Forces is counted and classified in only one group. The sum of the employed and the unemployed constitutes the civilian labor force. Persons not in the labor force combined with those in the civilian labor force constitute the civilian noninstitutional population 16 years of age and over. Under these concepts, most people are quite easily classified. For example:

- Elizabeth Lloyd reported to the interviewer that last week she worked 40 hours as a sales manager for the Western Beverage Company.
- Steve Hogan lost his job when the local plant of the Chariot Aircraft Manufacturing Company was closed down. Since then, he has been visiting the personnel offices of the other factories in the town trying to find a job.

- Linda Coleman is a homemaker. Last week, she was occupied with her normal household chores. She neither held a job nor looked for a job. Her 80 year old father who lives with her has not worked or looked for work because of a disability.

Each of these examples is clear cut. Elizabeth is employed; Steve is unemployed; and Linda and her father are not in the labor force.

Who Is Counted as Employed?

Not all of the wide range of job situations in the American economy fit neatly into a given category. For example, people are considered employed if they did any work at all for pay or profit during the survey week. This includes all part-time and temporary work, as well as regular full-time year-round employment. Persons also are counted as employed if they have a job at which they did not work during the survey week because they were:

- On vacation;
- Ill;
- Experiencing childcare problems;
- Taking care of some other family or personal obligation;
- On maternity or paternity leave;
- Involved in an industrial dispute; or
- Prevented from working by bad weather.

These persons are counted among the employed and tabulated separately as "with a job but not at work," because they have a specific job to which they will return.

But what about the two following cases?

George Lewis is 16 years old, and he has no job from which he receives any pay or profit. However, George does help with the regular chores around his father's farm about 20 hours each week.

Lisa Fox spends most of her time taking care of her home and children, but, all day Friday and Saturday, she helps in her husband's computer software store.

Under the Government's definition of employment, both George and Lisa are considered employed. They fall into a group called "unpaid family workers," which includes any person who worked 15 hours or more in a week without pay in a family-operated enterprise. Such persons contribute significantly to our productive effort and are an important part of our labor supply, particularly in agriculture and retail trade. However, unpaid family workers who work fewer than 15 hours per week are counted as "not in the labor force."

Who Is Counted as Unemployed?

Persons are classified as unemployed if they do not have a job, have actively looked for work in the prior 4 weeks, and are currently available for work. Actively looking for work may consist of any of the following activities:

- Contacting:
  - An employer directly or having a job interview;
  - A public or private employment agency;
  - Friends or relatives;
  - A school or university employment center;
- Sending out resumes or filling out applications;
- Placing or answering advertisements;
- Checking union or professional registers; or
- Some other means of active job search.

Passive methods of job search do not result in job seekers actually contacting potential employers, and therefore are not acceptable for classifying persons as unemployed. These would include such things as attending a job training program or course or merely reading the want ads.

Workers expecting to be recalled from layoff are counted as unemployed, whether or not they have engaged in a specific job-seeking activity. But, in all other cases, the individual must be actively engaged in some job search activity and available for work (except for temporary illness).

ACTIVITIES AND EXERCISES

1. In the article about cross-cultural television watching, Liebes says that she interviewed "second generation Americans living in Los Angeles." Why do you think she wanted to talk only with *second generation* Americans?

2. It is frequently argued that the media are liberal. You have been hired to determine empirically whether the media are liberal or conservative. For purposes of this assignment, you will define "the media" as mainstream news production. You can decide if you are going to look at the press or at television and adjust your operationalizations accordingly. You have to define and then operationalize the terms "liberal" and "conservative."

3. "In seeking to explain the variation in workers' wages, economists do not generally include differences in physical appearance as a reason, perhaps because physical appearance seems unrelated to labor productivity. However, social psychologists, sociologists, and management researchers have long argued that a person's looks affect how he or she is perceived and treated by others. With few exceptions their empirical studies support this contention; physically attractive individuals receive more favorable treatment than less attractive persons" (Loh, 1993, p. 420).

   How would you study this? What would your variables be? What would you be trying to explain, and what would you be using as your explanation? How would you operationalize the variables?

NOTE

1. This was an operationalization developed by students in a mass media course.

4

SAMPLING:

Where to Look for Answers

One of the areas of communication that interests many scholars is the way we justify ourselves. What sort of excuses do we make for our behavior? To what extent do we continuously redefine or rationalize our actions so that we are always, or nearly always, right?

Let's imagine you are interested in this aspect of communication and you decide to study it. You carefully watch your best friend for a week, and then, on the basis of your observations, you write a paper about justifications and present it at the International Communication Association's annual conference. The title of your paper is "Justification in the 1990s: An Empirical Look." When you finish your presentation, a member of the audience stands and says, "I think you have a serious sampling problem."

What do you think this means? What is wrong with the study described above?

SAMPLES

When you receive a sample of a commercial product, you expect that the tiny bottle of shampoo or mouthwash or breakfast cereal is *representative* of the actual product that you would purchase. It would be unfair, for example, if the sample of breakfast cereal you received in the mail was produced with ingredients of much higher quality than the product regularly available at the market. To produce a sample of one quality and a product of another would be misleading.

The same is true of sampling in the social sciences. The sample must look like what it is supposed to represent. We cannot study everyone, at all times, in all places. Instead, we study some specific group of people at some specific location at some specific time. And we argue that the information we obtain by doing this is *generalizable* to most people (or similar people) at other times and other places.

To say that some statement is *generalizable* means that if it is true or accurate for the sample then it is true or accurate for some larger group. And it is the larger group in which we are interested. The smaller group *represents* the larger group.

When 947 people are interviewed over the telephone about their confidence in the president, for example, no one really cares about those 947 people except to the extent that they are believed to be representative of the American people. The 947 people interviewed make up the *sample,* and the American people make up the *population.* The sample represents the population. What we can say about the sample is *generalizable* to the population.

Sources of the Sample

How confident would you be about the results of this Presidential Confidence Survey if you found out that the 947 people were found at a Woodstock reunion? Do you think that these people would be representative of all Americans? What if the sample were found at a Republican convention? A Democratic conven-

SIDEBAR 4.1 Excerpt from Robert Zussman's *Mechanics of the Middle Class: Work and Politics Among American Engineers* (1985, p. 30)

The Interview Sample

Before selecting particular individuals for interviews, I had to decide who I would count as an "engineer." This was not as simple a decision as it might at first seem. One procedure, used in one major national survey of engineers, would have included only individuals with four-year engineering degrees. However, this procedure would seriously distort a major intention of my study by defining the population in terms of educational level rather than by a position in the industrial division of labor. Indeed, the interplay between educational qualifications and position in the division of labor . . . is a major focus of arguments about proletarianization and professionalization. . . . Consequently, I adopted a different procedure for this study, selecting the sample from a population including 1) individuals with four-year degrees in engineering or related fields, not occupying primarily managerial or administrative positions, and 2) additional individuals, regardless of degree level, occupying positions requiring skills roughly equivalent to those occupied primarily by degreed engineers.

tion? An exclusive country club or an unemployment office? What if all 947 people interviewed were women? Or men? Or elderly? Or young? Or convicts? Or Baptists? Or suburban dwellers? Or members of the National Rifle Association? Or members of a gay rights organization?

These would not be good samples because there are obvious—and obviously relevant—differences between the people in the sample and the people in the population. A perfectly good sample of Baptists makes a perfectly bad sample of Americans—and that is true for all the groups mentioned above.

Let's go back to the example used at the beginning of this chapter and see what is wrong with having your friend serve as the sole source of information about "justification in the 1990s."

- There is no reason to think that your friend is representative of all human beings.
- The sample is far too small. You cannot use *one* person to look for *general* tendencies. All of us have our quirks and idiosyncrasies, so a sample that is too small is likely to be biased in odd ways.
- The title of the paper is "Justification in the 1990s." This implies that the way people justify themselves in the 1990s is different from the way people justified themselves in previous decades. The sample, however, provides no information about earlier decades that can serve as the basis for the implied comparison. If you are trying to establish that there have been *changes* in the way people justify their behavior, then it is necessary to document the change. If you do not do this with data, you can do it with references to earlier studies. If you do not mean to imply that there is something different about the 1990s, then the title should be amended to *Justification: An Empirical Look.*

These three weaknesses can be called, respectively, the problem of *representativeness,* the problem of *sample size,* and the problem of *fit.* We will look at each of these in turn, keeping in mind that the purpose of sampling is to design a sample in such a way that it is possible to look at a small group of people to draw conclusions about a larger group of people.

Representativeness

There are basically two ways to ensure that the people in your sample are representative of the people about whom you wish to generalize. The first is to attempt to *match* the people in the sample to the people in the population. That should be fairly obvious.

To do this, you need to decide which variables are relevant and then design your sample in such a way that the proportions in the sample match (or approximate) the proportions in the population. The second way is to *randomly select* people from the population. A random selection of subjects from a population should end up looking very much like the population.

If, for example, you were going to do a study of student attitudes on your campus, you might think that you would want to take a number of variables into consideration. For example, because the easiest way to get survey data on students is to pass out questionnaires in classrooms and because the largest classes are lower division classes, you would want to try to avoid having freshmen dominate your sample. Your reasoning would be that because college students are (hopefully) both learning and maturing it would be reasonable to expect the opinions of seniors to be different from those of freshmen. My brother once said that the difference between a first-semester college freshmen and a high school senior is a summer at the beach, but the difference between a senior and a freshman is 3 years of education, experience, and maturation.

Another variable that may make a difference is sex: The male experience is considerably different from the female experience, so you may want to match your sample to the population. Other variables that may be relevant are race and ethnicity, traditional/nontraditional students, and major.

If you are trying to match the sample to the population, it is necessary to know something about the population. If we want to have the proportion of females in the sample the same as the proportion of females in the population, then we need to know what that proportion is.

There are other ways to get representation. Imagine, for example, that you want to compare traditional to nontraditional students (nontraditional students are generally defined as undergraduates over the age of 25). Using entirely fictitious data, let's say that 65% of the student body on your campus are traditional students. You don't have to have traditional students make up

Table 4.1 The Student Population

	Women	Men	Total
Traditional students	2,000	1,750	3,750
Nontraditional students	1,500	500	2,000
Total	3,500	2,250	5,750

65% of your sample because you are not trying to get a sample that is representative of the entire student body. (Never lose sight of what you are talking about!) Instead, you want roughly the same number of traditional and nontraditional students: The actual number of students you want in your sample depends on the kind of research you are doing and how much time and money you have. What you need is a sample that represents each of the two groups.

Currently, about 60% of undergraduates in America are female. One possible reason for this overrepresentation of women is that there is an increase in returning, nontraditional students and more of them are women. Let's imagine that your campus looks like the one described in Table 4.1.

You can see that traditional students make up 65% of the student population (the number of traditional students divided by the total number of students, or $3,750/5,750 = .6521$). You can also see that 53% of the traditional students are women, whereas 75% of the nontraditional students are women. This means that if representative samples of traditional and nontraditional students are developed, any comparison of the two groups will have to take into consideration that the samples will not be matched by gender. This means you will have to ask yourself how much of the difference you found is due to the traditional/nontraditional difference and how much is due to the sex difference.

If you think gender might be an important variable (which it would be if you were interested, say, in sexual harassment or the

Table 4.2 A Purposive Sampling Design

	Women	Men	Total
Traditional students	100	100	200
Nontraditional students	100	100	200
Total	200	200	400

impact of family obligations or anything else that affects one gender more than the other), then you might want to create samples with equal numbers of traditional and nontraditional students *and* equal numbers of men and women. Such a sample is shown in Table 4.2.

These proportions look nothing at all like the proportions of the population. Instead of 65% traditional students, we have 50%. Instead of 9% of the students being nontraditional men (the number of nontraditional men divided by the total number of students, or 500/5,750 = .0869), a full 25% of the sample is made up of nontraditional male students.

If the sample is so different from the population, how can we say it is representative of the population? In terms of proportions, the sample is not even representative of the *subpopulations* of traditional and nontraditional students. Keep in mind what your purpose is, which in this case is a comparison of traditional and nontraditional students, *not* a description of the population and *not* a comparison of a group evenly divided between men and women with a group composed mostly of women. Having equal numbers of men and women and traditional and nontraditional students allows for comparisons to be made without their being biased by disproportionate groups.

The question to be asked of the sample above is how the 400 people were chosen out of the total student population of, say, 6,000. The best answer is that the sample was *randomly chosen.* Random selection of subjects (called *simple random sampling*) is the ideal on which statistical analysis is based. The second best answer is that the sample selection was *systematic*. The next best answer is that it was some sort of *convenience* sample. All of these will be discussed later in the book. All that is needed to know at this stage is that one does not stack the sample in one's favor or allow any major bias to creep into the sample.

Sample Size

How many people should you have in your sample? The answer is "As many as you need." How many you need depends on what you are going to do, so the bulk of the discussion of sample size will occur in the chapters on each methodology. There are, however, a few basic things to keep in mind:

- You never need a certain *proportion* of the population.
- There is always a point of diminishing returns when the cost of adding additional people has less and less of a payoff.
- The size of the sample is less important than the representativeness of the sample.
- Ideals aside, the biggest determinants of sample size are time and money.

One of the ways to think about sample size involves the concept of *sampling error*. Sampling error is based on the idea that no matter how good a sample is, it is never exactly the same as the population. The concept of sampling error accepts that samples differ from the population and that no two samples are ever going to be exactly alike.

You may hear newscasters talk about "sampling error" or the "margin of error" when discussing public opinion sampling. They will say things like, "Seventy-five percent of Americans do not know where the Korean War was fought, and 59% cannot name the year in which the War of 1812 occurred. The margin of error is plus or minus 3%."

Sampling error is based on a number of assumptions. First, the sample should be a *random* or a *systematic* sample. Second, this is

Table 4.3 Sampling Error

	Number of Interviews in Sample or Subgroup						
Percentages Near	2,000	1,500	1,000	600	400	200	100
5% or 95%	1	1	2	2	3	4	5
10% or 90%	2	2	2	3	4	5	7
20% or 80%	2	3	3	4	5	7	10
35% or 65%	3	3	4	5	6	8	12
50%	3	3	4	5	6	9	12

generally used with questions that are dichotomous, which means they are the kinds of questions that can be reduced to such answers as yes/no, for/against, or know/don't know.

Sometimes you will hear newscasters say that an election campaign is "too close to call" on the basis of the available survey data. Imagine that a survey of 1,000 people has been conducted and that 49% of the people responding say they will vote for Mr. Nice, whereas 51% say they will vote for Mr. Tough. Look at Table 4.3 at the line that says "50%." We look at this line because the percentages of the voters that are responding (49% and 51%) are closer to 50% than to any of the other numbers in that column. On that line, look in the column labeled "1,000" because that is the size of the survey, and you will see the number 4. This means there is a margin of error of plus or minus 4%. In other words, given a sample size of 1,000, in the *population* as few as 43% (47% minus 4%) or as many as 51% (47% plus 4%) might want to vote for Mr. Nice. It also means that as few as 49% or as many as 57% might favor Mr. Tough. Because there is an overlap between the highest possible support for Mr. Nice (51%) and the lowest possible support for Mr. Tough (49%), our data are not strong enough to predict who will win: The election is "too close to call."

Table 4.3 shows us two things. First, the finer the distinctions we are trying to make, the larger the sample size we will want. So the example I used put us around the 50-50 division, which is the best starting point to assume when you do not know how people will answer a question. When there is a substantial difference (e.g., a 90-10 split), a larger sample makes little difference for the margin of error: You can get plus or minus four percentage points with only 600 respondents. The second thing you have to notice is that to cut your margin of error in half you have to quadruple your sample size. Using the 50-50 division, quadrupling the sample size from 100 to 400 reduces the margin of error from 12 to 6, and quadrupling again, from 400 to 1,600, cuts the margin of error from 6 to 3. (The margin-of-error percentages are rounded, so a sample size of 1,500 approximates a margin of error of three percentage points.) This means that reducing the margin of error is expensive. After a certain sample size, there is no point in trying to reduce the margin of error. At what point we say the sample is large enough depends on personal judgment: Some go as low as 600 (which accounts for most commercial polls), and almost everyone agrees that going beyond 1,500 to 2,000 respondents is not cost-effective. We will talk about this again when we get to Chapter 8 on survey research.

The Question of Fit

The most important thing about a sample is that it can provide an answer to the question you are asking. To a great extent this is a matter of representativeness and size, but there is also a logical problem. In the example, a comparison was being made without reference to an earlier data set. Sometimes the comparison can be made using earlier research. Far too often, however, studies are published or presented with implied comparisons when the only comparison that is made is between the data and a bunch of stereotypical notions. If you want to know, for instance, how African Americans perceive political institutions, you need to know how people other than African Americans perceive them.

If you want to know how women feel about their career opportunities, you have to know how men feel about their career
opportunities.

Imagine that you were interested in how women felt about
their career opportunities, so you interviewed 150 women and
then concluded that "women think this and that about their career opportunities." How do you know that this is not how all
workers feel about their career opportunities? If you try to explain the findings of your study using gender, you could be entirely off base. Unless you look at how men feel, you'll have no
idea if what women feel is uniquely female or if it is something
they have in common with men. You need some empirical basis
for making empirical claims about comparison groups.

This is true of all group comparisons. Of course, if all you are
concerned with is how women think and you are not going
to make any claims that they think this way *because they are
women,* then you do not need a comparison group. This could be
the case, for example, if you were designing a marketing campaign for a product or service intended for women.

PROBABILITY SAMPLING

Sampling designs can be categorized into two basic types: probability and nonprobability.

A *probability sample* is one in which everyone in the population has a *known, nonzero chance* of being included in the sample. A *nonprobability sample* is any sample in which there is *not* a
known, nonzero chance of being included. This may sound more
complicated than it really is.

Imagine that I want to talk about Stanislaus County voters (my
population) and the voter registration list (my *sampling frame*)
indicates there are 50,000 voters in the county. If I drop all
50,000 names into a hat (or a computer) and blindly (*randomly*)
choose 1,000 names (my *sample*), then I have drawn a probability sample. It is a probability sample because everyone in the

population has a known, nonzero chance of being included. This chance is known as the *probability* of inclusion. In this case, the probability that any one voter will be chosen is 1 in 50. Expressed as probability, that is .02 (1,000 divided by 50,000). (Point oh-two means 2 in 100, and the convention is that probability is expressed as the chances of *one* thing happening. So "1 in 50" sounds better than "2 in 100.")

Let's go back to the study that started this chapter. You were looking at how people justify themselves, and you gathered your data by looking at how your friend behaved. This is a non-probability sample because people other than your friend had no chance of being chosen. People in far-off areas had zero chance of being included, and your friend was chosen because he or she was *convenient.* Nonprobability samples are often called *convenience* samples.

But let's imagine that your research design includes talking with someone at great length and following people around in or-der to watch them actually interact with other people. This sort of design is so time and labor intensive that the sample size is proba-bly going to be quite small—possibly as small as 20 people. The question becomes: How do you choose 20 people out of a popula-tion of hundreds of millions (Americans) or even billions (inhab-itants of earth)? The short answer is: not easily. The more com-plex answer is that it depends on what you want to find out.

NONPROBABILITY SAMPLING

Sometimes probability sampling is not possible. There can be a number of reasons for this, ranging from practical (lack of time, money, or available sample frames) to social (some groups are hard to gain access to). Though probability sampling is generally considered the best, it cannot be used as the standard if it is either inappropriate or impossible.

In the early 1990s, I was part of a team researching various health care aspects of the AIDS epidemic. One morning, I read in

> **SIDEBAR 4.2 Some Thoughts on Probability Sampling:**
> **What *Everyone* Means**
>
> You have to keep in mind that when we say that everyone in a population has to have a known, nonzero chance of being included, we really don't mean *everyone*.
>
> It is generally accepted that random telephone dialing can reach the population, but we all know that there are people without telephones. There are people without addresses. There are criminals on the lam, hiding under false names. There are out-of-date voter registration lists and incomplete membership lists. This means that most, but not all, members of a population can be found in a probability sampling frame.
>
> There are really two separate problems. One problem is whether the population you are seeking is really the population you are claiming to get. There is not an exact match between the population of people with phones—or people with addresses—and people who live in this country. But for most purposes, you will act as if they were the same. And, of course, you will tell the audience that you used phones or mail so that it will be clear what you are doing. The second problem concerns the match between your sampling frame (your source of information) and the population of people you can reach. This means if you accept that you can reach only people with phones, you still have to figure out a way to get them. The phone book, as we all know, excludes lots of people because many people have opted for unlisted numbers. The match, then, between the phone book as a sampling frame and the population you are trying to reach is not a good one. Random-digit dialing (which will be discussed in Chapter 8) is a much better way of giving everyone an opportunity to participate in the study you are conducting.

the paper that a national convention of nurse practitioners was beginning the following morning in a local hotel. Nurse practitioners are interesting in the context of HIV because, like nurses, they have lots of patient contact and, like physicians, they can act as the primary caregiver. We immediately revised some survey questionnaires that had been designed for physicians and dentists and adapted them to nurse practitioners. I called the association responsible for the convention and got permission to blanket the convention site with questionnaires.

This was not the ideal way to study a professional group, but at the same time it was an opportunity we did not want to pass up. The convention provided an opportunity to get a great deal of information in a short period of time at a very low cost. We felt that regardless of the strategy's imperfections we should take advantage of the convention. This sort of sampling is known as *opportunity* or *convenience* sampling.

Probability sampling is required for most statistical analysis. This is because the idea of probability is the underlying assumption in statistical mathematics. Because of this, probability sampling designs will be discussed in the chapters on experimentation (Chapter 7), surveys (Chapter 8) and, to a certain extent, content analysis (Chapter 9). Nonprobability sampling is generally associated with qualitative (nonmathematical) methods like fieldwork and will be discussed in Chapter 6).

SUMMARY

Sampling can become very complex, and it manifests itself differently in each of the methodologies we discuss. The important thing to keep in mind is that, for the most part, when we study anything in the social sciences we do so with the hope that what we find out will be generalizable to the larger world. We study some relationships, corporations, movies, or news stories to get some general understanding of all (or most) relationships, corporations, movies, or news stories.

This means that you have to choose carefully what you study. What you study has to be fairly typical to be representative. You have to study enough things (people, organizations, days, situa-

SIDEBAR 4.3 Vocabulary

Convenience sample	Generalize	Nonprobability sample
Population	Probability sample	Random sample
Representative	Sample	Sample error
Snowball sample	Systematic sample	

tions, objects, etc.) to get past the inevitable uniqueness of individuality. And you have to make sure that the sample you have chosen can actually provide an answer to the question you want to ask.

ACTIVITIES AND EXERCISES

1. You want to look at gender differences in communication among college students. What is your population? What sort of sample would you use if you wanted to have 500 students fill out a questionnaire?
2. You want to conduct a study of job satisfaction among whites and minorities. How would you go about getting a sample? How would you learn about job satisfaction?

5

WRITING THE RESEARCH PAPER:

Research Methodology as a Rhetorical Strategy

RESEARCH METHODOLOGY AND RHETORICAL STRATEGY

As already discussed, formalized research methodology serves two purposes. The first is to keep us, as researchers, honest and able to control our biases and reduce our errors. The second is to enable us to convince a skeptical audience that what we have found is valid and accurate. It is this second aspect of research methodology that makes it a rhetorical strategy.

Someone once referred to the prose used in research journal articles as the "no-style style." By this, it was meant that "scientific" writing lacked the personal idiosyncrasies and stylistic flourishes associated with a more literary or poetic style of writing. But scientific writing, of course, does not lack style. Instead, it has a very formal style that was developed as part of a deliberate effort to remove the writer from the writing and to make science seem as impersonal as possible. Impersonality was (and is) associated with objectivity, and objectivity is one of the qualities associated with the scientific idea of facts, proof, and truth. For this reason, researchers tend to remove personal pronouns and to write in straightforward, matter-of-fact sentences. This is also the reason for the sometimes excessive number of citations in social science articles: Ideas must be seen as coming from anywhere except the personal beliefs and experiences of the person actually doing the research. There is a deliberate distancing of the individual from the work and an equally deliberate effort to establish a connection with a community of scholars and with a tradition of research.

There is some tension between these two aspects of research methodology. The first is concerned with truth, honesty, accuracy, impartiality, and objectivity. The second—well, the second is concerned with *rhetoric,* and rhetoric seems concerned with none of these things. Rhetoric is about words and persuasion; it is about convincing people of things, about selling them ideas, and about creating logical illusions. Rhetoric is the art of using language effectively and persuasively. In contrast, the ideals of science posit a means of knowing that supposedly bypasses language altogether, going directly from the world to the brain via first-hand experience. And, even worse, rhetoric is associated with *art,* whereas science is, obviously, *science. Science* is serious, whereas *art* is frivolous; science is factual, whereas art is fictional; science is about reality, whereas art is about perceptions and feelings. The famous observation is that science and art divide humanity between those of us who are hard-headed and those who are soft-hearted.

Science, then, is aligned *against* the rhetorical approach to rationality. At the same time, however, we describe our research methodology to our audience in order to let them know how much they can trust what we are telling them. In this sense, the methodology sections of a research article are performing a rhetorical function. In the beginning of this text, I said that the goal of research is not to convince people who already believe (or have a tendency to believe) what you want to tell them but to convince skeptics and opponents. *Convincing* is a form of persuasion, and persuasion is the goal of rhetoric.

Research methodology is an antirhetorical strategy—which is itself a rhetorical strategy. As researchers, we are saying, in effect, "You should not believe what I am saying because I can wrap it up in fine, flowery phrases. You should not believe what I tell you because I can bamboozle you with subtly shifting definitions and overly convoluted terminology. Instead, you should believe what I say because I can show you, plainly and clearly, what I have done and the basis from which my conclusions follow." The idea of plain, clear reasoning on the basis of evidence is a rhetorical strategy.

BUILDING ARGUMENTS

Even though we are engaged in empirical research, we are building an argument just as if we were talking about politics, philosophy, religion, or aesthetics. The difference is that we are merging logic and evidence and are spending a lot of time ensuring that our evidence is seen *as evidence* rather than as purely logical moves. This means that when we write about empirical research we are building three arguments simultaneously:

1. A methodological argument about the *status* of our empirical evidence
2. An analytic argument about the *meaning* of that evidence
3. A logical argument about the *relationships* between our concepts

By *status of the empirical evidence,* I mean the means by which the data were collected: Are the data trustworthy? Are the data reliable and valid? By *meaning,* I am referring to the interpretation of the data. By *relationships,* I mean the validity of the connections between the ideas, the research, and the interpretations.

An argument is like a trail that we want others to follow. This means that all of our directions, signposts, and transition points must be clear. Our point is not to make a pretty trail or one that is attractive because it is unique and quirky. The goal in an argument is to let the audience follow us from the starting point to the ending point without ever feeling lost, confused, or abused.

THE FORMAL STYLE

The formal style of writing research reports is a crucial part of the research culture. And if it is an intrinsic part of the research activity, then it is one that we must master. Think of the idea of *rhetorical sensitivity.* Rhetorical sensitivity is the tendency to present material to people in a way they can understand. This means that the way one talks with small children is not the same as the way one talks with one's adult peers. The way one goes about convincing someone of a theological point is not the same as the way one goes about convincing someone of an empirical point. The strategies are different, the audiences are different. One purpose of intentional communication is to get your ideas across— to let people see what you are trying to say. To do this, you use the conventions peculiar to the audience you are trying to reach. Formal empirical research is a culturally defined activity and also an activity that defines a culture—or at least a subculture. The formal style is the rhetorically sensitive approach in the research culture.

So you have to learn the rationale of the formal style used in science.

WRITING AN EMPIRICAL PAPER

An empirical paper consists of the following parts, which usually appear in this order:

Conceptual Elements	Methodological Elements	Conceptual Elements
Theory	Hypotheses	Analysis
Review of the Literature	Operationalization of Terms	Conclusion
		Implications
	Design	
	Sample	
	Findings	

The *conceptual elements* tell the reader what your ideas are and how your ideas relate to what other scholars are thinking.

The *methodological elements* tell the reader how you are going to research your ideas. I put "findings" in this section, although it is an odd fit. The methodology section lays out your research plan and your rationale. The "findings" are what you find after implementing that plan.

In the conceptual elements section, the *analysis* tells the reader what you think the findings mean, the *conclusion* tells the readers how the analysis relates back to your ideas in your theory section, and the *implications* section discusses ways your conclusions can be expanded or supported.

Or, put another way, a research paper looks like this:

1. This is what I've been thinking about. (*theory*)
2. This is what other people have said about what I've been thinking about. (*review*)
3. This is what I think I would find if I looked to test my ideas. (*hypotheses*)
4. By the way, when I say "X," I mean this and that. (*operationalization*)
5. This is my plan for looking. (*design*)
6. These are the kinds of people, places, and things I am going to look at. (*sample*)
7. This is what I found out. (*findings*)

8. This is what the findings mean. (*analysis*)

9. This is how what I found relates to the ideas I had at the beginning. (*conclusion*)

10. Given all this, I think we should look at. . . .(*implications*)

We will look at each of these in turn.

CONCEPTUAL ELEMENTS

Even in the most descriptive research projects, the researcher has some *reason* to examine the part of life that forms his or her subject matter. The subject was not chosen arbitrarily. Even when research is designated as "exploratory," there is some reason why *this* is being explored rather than something else. The subtitle of this book refers to the rules of *looking,* not the rules of *seeing,* because looking is not a passive process. It requires some effort. Some methodologies and some topics will entail more conceptualizations than others, but all methodologies and topics require some.

Theories

A theory is an attempt to explain or represent some aspect of reality. Theories are abstract, in the sense that they do not refer to some concrete, immediately testable reality. Famous theories include the theory of relativity and the theory of evolution. These are grand theories, often called "macro-level theories" because they are so all-encompassing. Macro-level theories in the social sciences include Marxism, symbolic interactionism, feminism, and systems theory, to name just a few. These theories—like all theories—cannot be tested directly, so they are neither true nor false. Rather, they are rich enough to create hypotheses that *can* be tested and found to be either valid or invalid. A theory must be capable of generating testable hypotheses (hypotheses will be

SIDEBAR 5.1 Formal Style Tip

Use of quotation marks indicates either that what follows is a direct quote (i.e., *exactly* what someone actually said or wrote) or that you do not really mean or believe what you are saying. An example of the latter is, "Today's 'educated' person quite often has no historical knowledge at all." There is almost an audible sneer involved in this use of quotes.

Quotation marks should not be used in place of either italics or underlines to indicate emphasis.

discussed in more detail later in this chapter); otherwise, it cannot be considered a scientific or social scientific theory. A theory that cannot be tested in this manner is a philosophical theory or a religious belief.[1]

For the most part, the theories that are used in empirical works have been generated elsewhere—in different articles or books, at an earlier time. Most of the theories used in communication research are fairly low level. They are not nearly as grand as theories of evolution, relativity, Marxism, or feminism.

In a recent edition of *Communication Monographs* (chosen only because it happened to be on my desk), only one of the four articles had anything that could even be considered a formal theory. Beatty, McCroskey, and Heisel (1998) posit a biological basis for communication anxiety, whereas the others explore what, at the most, could be considered "ideas:" that the hurtfulness of a remark is dependent on the relationship of the speaker and hearer (Vangelisti & Crumley, 1998), that people in the semiconductor industry volunteered to adopt standards (Browning and Beyer, 1998), and that many of the groups using parliamentary procedures do not really understand them very well (Weitzel & Geist, 1998).

This does not mean that theories are not used in setting up the problem. Vangelisti and Crumley (1998), for example, are look-

SIDEBAR 5.2 Formal Style Tip

Do not use contractions. Contractions are an indication of informal writing. Most research reports are formal. They are used in either business or academics. So do not say *don't*, *isn't* is not appropriate, and *won't* will not do.

ing at the role of relationships in interpreting hurtful remarks. They tell us that "theorists suggest that relationships serve as a backdrop for how individuals interpret and react to communication" (p. 173) and that "the qualities of interpersonal associations—including closeness, satisfaction, and history—affect the way partners perceive and respond to social interaction" (p. 173). These are theoretical remarks because they are abstract—too general to be put directly to the test. Vangelisti and Crumley test these remarks by focusing on hurtful remarks: "More specifically, the associations between various relational qualities and responses to hurtful messages were investigated, as was the possible influence of particular types of relationships (e.g., those between family members or romantic partners) on people's reactions to hurt" (p. 174).

Let's take a careful look at the statements made in the previous paragraph. Vangelisti and Crumley say that theorists are telling us that the meaning of a remark (or of an interaction) does not take place solely in the brain of the person who hears the remark. Instead, the meaning is determined in the (social, historical, interpersonal) context in which it was made, and one of the important contexts for any remark is the relationship between the person making it and the person receiving it. This is the first sentence quoted in the previous paragraph. The second quote moves this idea forward by saying that it is not just the relationship that matters but the qualities of the relationship. The authors mention the qualities of "closeness, satisfaction, and history." You may be

SIDEBAR 5.3 Formal Style Tip

There are two basic rules on numbers. First, numbers one through nine are written as words, not as numerals, and numbers greater than nine are written as numerals, not as words. Second, no matter what the number, if it is used to begin a sentence, it must be written as a word.

someone's friend, but that does not mean that you are *close* friends, that you are completely satisfied with the relationship, or that you have been friends for a long time. These things make a difference. Or so Vangelisti and Crumley are arguing.

So far this is theoretical because it is all so general. It is about *all* communication, *all* relationships, *all* qualities of *all* relationships, and *all* possible interactions. You have to ask yourself what it means—what the world would look like if these ideas were true. Vangelisti and Crumley conduct research to determine if you can apply these ideas to one particular kind of communication. Philosophers tend to talk about *factual statements* a great deal, but those who look at people actually talking understand that making factual remarks is only one of the many things we do when we communicate. And making factual statements is one of the more bloodless, uninteresting things that we do. How, Vangelisti and Crumley ask, would these ideas about the role of context apply to *hurting* people? Hmmm, now *that* could be interesting.

Theories as Hooks

In many ways, this idea that the relationship between two people determines the meaning (to those people) of the messages they exchange is commonsensical. If your best friend, laughing, calls you an idiot, it is very different than if your boss, stern-faced, calls you an idiot: The meaning is not the same. On the other hand, it is also quite a *big* idea: Vangelisti and Crumley are exploring the idea of meaning within commonplace settings. Is meaning found in the speaker's intentions, in the audience's perception, or in the "message itself"?

If anyone asks Vangelisti and Crumley why their work is interesting—why, that is, is it important enough to bother reading—they can cite their theoretical basis. It does not matter, then, if you really do not care about hurtful remarks because this study is one small empirical test of a huge theoretical project concerning the idea of meaning. It does not matter why Vangelisti and Crumley are interested in hurtful remarks. It may be that they have both just come out of bad relationships or are from abusive families or that they cannot understand why some people are so nasty to others. That may be their *motivation* for being interested, but it is not why the article is (or is not) interesting.

This means that when you write a paper and tell us why we should be interested in reading it, you should not tell us your personal reasons for being interested in the topic. It is very likely that we will not share them. Instead, tell us why the research is interesting *in itself.* This does not mean that the research will be interesting to everyone; rather, it means that it will be interesting to anyone who studies meaning or relationships, or perhaps to people interested in family therapy, the social construction of reality, or symbolic interactionism.

The theoretical introduction to a paper tell us why it is interesting. Do not start with a sentence that reads, "I think it is interesting because. . . ." It is not interesting because you think it is; rather, you think it is interesting because it has some qualities: It links to other ideas, or it provides a novel way of looking at things, a new slant on old ideas, or the opportunity to clarify something. So tell us about these qualities. A research report is a formal paper, and this means that one needs to be as objective as possible. By *objective,* I mean taking into consideration views other than one's own. It may be interesting, for example, to find out why Sigmund Freud was so interested in sex, but Freud's work is interesting because it touches on ideas, questions, and sentiments that we have all have had. We do not have to know anything about Freud, nor do we have to agree with his arguments, to concede that his work is interesting.

Vangelisti and Crumley's opening sentence is: "Even in the closest, most satisfying relationships, people sometimes say things that hurt each other" (p. 173). They do not hedge this by saying, "*We think* that even in the closest . . ." or "*It seems to us* that even in the closest. . . ." You should not use these sorts of "weasel words" either. We know that this is what Vangelisti and Crumley think because Vangelisti and Crumley's names are at the top of the paper. "Weasel words" rob the statement of impact and strength. There is a time to be careful and modest about the claims one is making, but the introductory sentences are not a good place: If you are not even sure of what you are saying, why should the reader continue?

In the first sentence of the second paragraph, Vangelisti and Crumley ask, "Why do hurtful interactions devastate some relationships and have little effect on others?" (p. 173). The first sentence establishes the universality of the behavior they are going to examine—that everyone makes hurtful remarks—and then this question leads them into their theoretical angle: that the nature of the relationship determines the meaning of the interaction.

This is a nice, formal beginning. This is the way you should begin your papers. There is a rule that states that in formal papers you should never use the first-person pronoun: a rule, that is, that you should never refer to yourself. Such rules can create awkward prose, but the point of the rule is to force writers to think in general terms, outside of themselves. This is a good rule to keep in mind. Some publications insist that there be no reference to the author's personal experience that is not couched in objective terms. But even if you are not writing for such publications, you should be careful about using *I, me,* and *we.* Ask yourself what purpose it serves. Ask yourself if the reader gets a clearer picture if the pronouns are used than if they are not.

The theory section of a research paper, then, provides the general conceptual framework for the research. This section tells the reader why the research is interesting or important by linking it to more general ideas. This is similar to the idea of a sample: We are not interested, necessarily, in the particular people we are studying. Rather, we are interested in the population that the sample represents. In an analogous fashion, we may not care at all about relationships or hurtful remarks, but we may care a great deal about the role of social context in communication, and this may provide one of the pieces of the puzzle—or change the way we have thought about previously collected pieces.

Review of the Literature

Intellectual effort is a social phenomenon. Isaac Newton wrote that he was able to accomplish what he did because he was "standing on the shoulders of giants." It is a wonderful image— both cooperative and competitive, dependent and transcending. There is nothing that any one of us is interested in that has not interested others before us. I remember as an undergraduate being frustrated by the realization that people dead for hundreds of years were stealing my ideas as fast as I could generate them. We do not think in a vacuum. We get our ideas from others, and we look to others to clarify or advance our thinking. When you get a research idea, you have to go to the library and find out what is already known about the topic. This is called "reviewing the literature." The "literature" refers to journal articles.

Journal articles are used because the research they present is generally more current than that published in books. This does not mean that you should not use books, but journal articles are the most current research reports available in most libraries.

A *journal* is an academic magazinelike periodical. (A list of communication journals can be found in Appendix B.) Unlike magazines, there is very little advertising (usually none) in academic journals. Such journals are usually produced by professional associations such as the National Communication

SIDEBAR 5.4 Formal Style Tip

The use of theories must be integrated into your arguments. Do not personalize or anthropomorphize theories. Do not say, for example, "Communicator Style says la de dah." There is no person named Communicator Style, and only persons can say things.

One student wrote: "This is explained in social construction theory . . ." This should be written more like: "According to Berger and Luckman (p. 137), structural explanations of human behavior . . ." or "Berger and Luckman claimed [argued, said, etc.] that structural explanations of human behavior . . ." (p. 137).

The purpose of a review of the literature is to *use* other people's work, not to report on it.

Association, the American Sociological Association, or the International Communication Association.

A review of the literature is conducted for a number of reasons:

- To find out (and incorporate) the most current theoretical thinking
- To place a question within a scholarly context
- To find out (and build on) the results of recent (and historical) empirical research
- To see how variables have traditionally been operationalized
- To find, borrow, and build on the research designs of others

In short, the review of the literature allows you to put your ideas into a scholarly context in order to clarify them and to allow you to build on what is already known. This section provides the knowledge and information required to move your ideas to the point where they can be tested empirically.

METHODOLOGICAL ELEMENTS

Operationalization of Terms

As discussed in Chapter 3, the point of operationalization is to let the reader know what you mean by key concepts. This is crucial. I think the oil that allows society to run smoothly is conceptual vagueness, aided by ambiguity. But here we are using the formal style, and we are deliberately trying *not* to slide our way over or around difficulties. Remember: Our rhetorical strategy is to avoid traditional rhetorical strategies and be as open and transparent as possible.

Operationalization, to refresh your memory, is designed to enable the researcher to tell the audience the decision rules for including some things and excluding others. Let us look at a few examples.

Example

William Kirkwood and Dan Brown (1995) wanted to look at the way people attributed responsibility for diseases in the United States. They were interested not in how the professional medical establishment thought about disease but rather in how the nonprofessional public thought about disease. So the question was rather vague. They thought "people" talked a certain way about medical issues. Well, who counts as "people"? What counts as "talk"? They say, "Following Fisher's (1987) definition of public argument, we *defined public communication about disease* [italics in original] as messages about the causes of disease directed to broadly defined, nontechnical audiences. We examined messages about cancer, heart disease, stroke, lung and pulmonary disease" (p. 173).

This definition lets you know which sorts of messages Kirkwood and Brown looked at as well as the topics the messages included. Thus, "messages about the causes of disease directed to broadly defined, nontechnical audiences" that were about psychological problems, acne, or ulcers were not included in the study. Now, what do they mean by "messages . . . to a broadly defined, nontechnical audience"? This needs to be operationalized. You could decide to operationalize this as mass media messages and then operationalize mass media messages as newspaper articles. Or you could look at television news stories or television news magazine stories or print magazine stories. Or you could look at books and pamphlets written by health care professionals for the general public, and this would take you to the health care sections in popular bookstores or to companies that publish patient education material.

No one expects you to look at everything or everyone. Let the reader or audience know what you looked at. Let the reader know what you are looking for in, for example, newspaper stories about health. Kirkwood and Brown discuss five rhetorical strategies: How do they know when they have found them in a given story? How would you know?

What to Operationalize

Beginning writers often do not know which concepts need to be operationalized. By the time you get to this section of your paper, you have already articulated your ideas and have related them to the work of other scholars. Your conceptualizations should be clear by this point. Your definitions should already be in place. By the end of the conceptualization, *it should be clear what you think.* Now you need only operationalize the concepts that clarify *what it is you are going to do.*

Operationalizations are designed to allow a member of your audience to understand what it is that you actually did. Kirkwood and Brown operationalized "public discussion of medical issues" as messages directed at average people and about specific diseases.

Think of the imaginary box used in the chapter on variables. It had sections for interrupters and noninterrupters. If I were going to conduct your research for you, what would I have to know to

SIDEBAR 5.5 Formal Style Tip

Notice that I refer to "Kirkwood and Brown" rather than "Professors Kirkwood and Brown" or "Drs. Kirkwood and Brown." Part of the formal style is to avoid any "argument by authority." That these two men are professors, have doctorate degrees, or may have some level of fame or multiple publications is irrelevant to the value of what they say. As a form of egalitarian respect, the first mention of the name gives the complete name (without title); after that, everyone is referred to using only the surname. It is a journalistic convention.

fill up the box the way you envision it being filled up? Where would I go? Who would I look at? What would count as a "group engaged in conversation"? What would count as an interruption—what would it *look* like?

I was engaged in research looking at poverty in a central California county. We had to decide what was meant by *poverty, underemployment, unemployment, unskilled, skilled, professional, technical labor, self-employed,* and the *underground economy*—not in the abstract, but in this way: Here are Bob, José, Susan, Vadim, and Rose. Is Bob unemployed? Yes or no? Is he underemployed? Yes or no? Why? What about Susan? What about Vadim? If you help your neighbor paint his fence and he lends you his lawnmower, do we count you as members of the underground economy? Yes or no, and why? What is the *rule* we are using for this?

This example shows the difference between a definition and an operationalization. If we define the underground economy as involving the "transfer of goods and services for goods, services, or money without reporting it to the government for purposes of taxation," that is a good, clear definition. It means that you are part of the underground economy if you fix someone's car or paint someone's house and get paid in cash. But what about the give and take between neighbors? "I'll help out with that addition you're building if you'll give me a hand with my car." In real life, it does not even have to be stated. If you allow your neighbor to help out all the time but you refuse to help him in return, then you are a bad neighbor; you aren't playing the game of neighborliness. So should we count such help as being part of the underground economy? Should we count 16-year-old baby-sitters as part of the underground? This is a decision that requires a rule, and that rule is your *operationalization* of the concept "underground economy."

You can see how a report on poverty needs to be very clear on these concepts. Politicians, who are not obligated to operationalize their terms, play fast and loose with the ideas such as "middle class" or "working poor." They do this so that they cannot be pinned down. We all tend to do the same thing in conversations with friends and relatives, at least sometimes, either because we have shared values or because we do not want to make our divisions obvious. If you do not operationalize such variables clearly, the readers will supply their own understanding, and this may or may not correspond with yours. You operationalize not so that people will agree with your understanding of a concept but so they may know what you are talking about, *regardless of whether they would operationalize it in a similar fashion.*

Keep in mind that you may not have to operationalize anything. You may be talking about something that is completely clear and self-evident—or at least is so by the time you have finished your theory and review of the literature sections. For example, you could look at the relationship between the gender of the teacher and the students' grade-point averages. In such a situation, gender is not a problematic concept. GPA is already an operationalization of student performance. You do not have to explain these things. If you were looking at the effect of student-teacher interactions on students' satisfaction, then you would have to operationalize what you mean by both student-teacher interactions and student satisfaction.

SIDEBAR 5.6 Formal Style Tip

The word *therefore* indicates that a deductive conclusion is about to be drawn. This is a very strong claim to make because a deductive conclusion indicates that the preceding argument is so tight that the conclusion must be accepted. Do not just throw this word around.

Hypotheses and Research Questions

Keep in mind: These are rules for *looking,* and when you are looking, you are looking *for* something.

Hypotheses

So far, we have this: You have told us what your ideas are, and you have shown us how those ideas relate to the work of other scholars. Then you have operationalized all the problematic concepts. Now you have to tell us what you expect to find.

You are not, after all, without any clue regarding what you will find when you look at the world. You have an idea, and a statement of that idea is your hypothesis. A clear hypothetical statement allows everyone to see exactly how strongly your ideas are supported by the research you have conducted.

Hypotheses are generally used in nomothetic (deductive, quantitative) methodologies, but some version of hypotheses are not out of place in any methodology.

Research Questions

If your ideas are not formulated in such a way that you can generate clear hypotheses, you can use research questions instead. In a research question, you clearly state the questions that inform your research. They could look like this:

Research Question 1: Do students who check out books from the library make better students?

Research Question 2: Do students who read fiction or non-academic material make better students?

Research questions and hypotheses are ways of letting your reader know exactly what you are looking for. Notice that a hypothesis is a *statement* about an expected relationship and a research question is, well, a *question.*

The Design

This is where you tell the reader what you actually did.

The design has to be clear enough that if someone wanted to replicate your work, it would be possible to do so. Present the design logically rather than chronologically. Quite often, students write along the lines of "First, I did this, then I did that." This is boring.

A few years ago, one of my students wanted to know what governed people's willingness to pick up coins off the ground. He thought there were two variables: the value of the coin and the potential for witnesses. He could have said this:

I put a penny near the front door of the supermarket, and I waited to see if anyone picked it up. Then I replaced the penny with a nickel, then a dime, and then a quarter. Then I put a penny on the edge of a card (so that it would be more visible against the blacktop) out in the market's parking lot. Then, I replaced the penny with a nickel, then a dime, and then a quarter.

Or he could have written:

The "public" location was a spot just to the right of the market door, and the "private" location was in the market parking lot. Because the parking lot surface was darker than the surface near the entrance to the market, the coin was placed half-way over the edge of a slightly dirtied 3 × 5 index card. The coins used were pennies, nickels, dimes, and quarters. At each location, each denomination was observed for 20 minutes, and. . . .

You can see that the first example is very personal and concrete. In contrast, the second example ties the behavior directly to the research ideas. The comparison that this student wanted to make was between how people acted in private and how they acted in public. It was not a comparison between what people did when the student did different things. The student could have had an assistant who placed the coins. As far as we are concerned, it doesn't matter who placed the coins. Our interest is what is meant by *public* and *private* in this context.

The design will vary from methodology to methodology. The point is to give the reader a clear picture of what you did to generate the results you found. I said above that an argument is like a trail. The problem is that if there are gaps in the trail, people will stop following you. Your ideas have to be linked to the appropriate literature. Your operationalizations have to be plausible. And your research design has to be capable of generating answers to the questions you are asking. At any point, your readers can leave you and the design portion of your report is a crucial spot. Any data you generate as a result of your activities are only as good as the design that shaped them. If you are vague or the design is inappropriate or sloppy, the data really will not have any value.

Students have a tendency to develop very creative research designs almost unrelated to any question they have formulated or to develop questions to fit the design. The problem with doing this is that it is immediately obvious. And it is backwards.

Sampling

The sample is an important part of the design. It may be the crucial part of the design. Getting an appropriate sample is usually just a matter of thinking very carefully about the population to which you want to generalize.

The description and explanation of your sampling design should be brief. A paragraph will usually be sufficient unless it is an amazingly complex design.

FINDINGS

What you actually found—your data—needs to be presented as objectively as possible. The goal in the formal style we have been discussing is to separate the presentation of the data from the analysis and interpretation of the data.

This means that here you back off in your writing. You distance yourself and content yourself with presenting data. This can be very difficult because the data are important only on the basis of the meaning they have for your study. There are a great many theorists and pessimists who say that this sort of separation is not possible. We do not have to worry about such people because, as researchers, we are committed to the idea that there is a distinction between finding something and saying what that something means.

There are two good reasons for keeping this separation. The first is that it makes it possible for people to accept your data as legitimate yet dismiss your analysis and interpretation as unwarranted. This separation also enables people to reinterpret your data and to compare your data with those of other studies.

The second reason has to do with that trail metaphor again. People who read a lot of research or who are dependent on research to make decisions are very critical people. This means that they feel capable of interpreting data on their own. It also means

that, as *critical* readers, they are trying to think of ways of rejecting your data. In group discussion courses, texts often talk about
people who engage in "silent arguing." In most group texts, silent
arguing is considered a bad thing to do, but in a world of information overkill we all have to develop strategies for sorting through
information. The idea of following the trail that I have been using
is meant to suggest that each transition point in the argument
must appear to be legitimate and that at each transition point
people who are unconvinced have a right to leave—to stop following you. And if they stop following you, you have wasted your
time.

The people who are following you are arguing against you. If
you have gone through a great deal of effort to set up and justify a
research project and the product of that research is only presented within an interpretive framework, you will lose your
readers.

CONCEPTUAL ELEMENTS

Analysis

The analysis of data is the section where you get to say what
your data mean. The key danger in this section is trying to make
your data carry more weight than they can possibly support. This
is known as "going beyond your data." Some general guidelines
are as follows.

When Analyzing Your Data, Never
Lose Sight of Your Question

The formal scientific style reinforces the idea that first you
think and then you look. The structure of the paper indicates that
you progressed in a linear manner from your theory to your conclusion. This means that each section must be driven by what has
been said in previous sections. If you suddenly start talking about

SIDEBAR 5.7 Formal Style Tip

Researchers rarely claim to *prove* things or to find out what is *true*. Instead, they say that their hypotheses were supported or not supported. The words *prove* and *true* have tremendous finality, and science is an ongoing activity. Scientists are methodologically quite humble and leave the idea of *proof* to mathematicians and logicians.

different questions or different variables, then you have broken the thread of the argument. This sometimes happens in quantitative analysis when suddenly one variable becomes unexpectedly powerful. In your analysis, you suddenly see gender, for example, as a tremendously important variable—but your original questions had nothing to do with gender.

Do not lose track of why you gathered the data. Focus on trying to answer the questions you have raised.

When Analyzing Your Data, Never Lose Sight of Your Sample

Remember where the data came from. A study of college students is not a study of Americans. Nor is it a study of "young people." It is probably only a study of certain kinds of college students: junior college students, elite university students, or private liberal arts college students, for example. A study of television commercials is not a study of Americans. It is not even a study of "the media," and certainly not a study of media owners or workers.

Look very critically at your sample. You chose it because it fit your needs. Do not warp it beyond what it was designed to do. A study of business owners and their values may be a study of middle-aged, middle-class, white Protestant men. A study of women may be a study of professional women or of white women.

SIDEBAR 5.8 Formal Style Tip

A research paper should be easily outlined. It helps, of course, to outline before you begin to write. Outlining afterwards is also very useful. Look at each paragraph and see how it fits into your presentation. Does it advance the argument you are making? Is it an interesting but irrelevant digression?

   Does the outline developed from the finished paper look like the outline you used in organizing your thoughts before you began writing? Do the changes, if any, make your presentation cleaner and more forceful, or do they make it more confusing and more difficult to follow?

When Analyzing Your Data, Never Lose Sight of Your Methodology

If you do an experiment, do not lose sight of the fact that it did not happen naturally. If you do a survey, do not lose sight of the fact that what you have as data are statements of values, beliefs, and intentions and not data about behaviors or actions. You have to work out the extent to which these survey statements reflect anything in reality. If you do fieldwork, remember that people act differently when they know they are being watched and that it is extraordinarily difficult to see past what we want to see. When doing content analysis, remember that you are not analyzing people.

Conclusion and Implications

The conclusion brings the research project full circle. How did what you found, in the larger sense of analyzed information, relate to what you wanted to know?

If your questions were not answered, tell us why they were not. If they were, tell us how. Tell us how it makes you change or refine your ideas. Tell us what you would like to do next: Which piece of the puzzle now seems important? Which population would you want to look at next?

NONACADEMIC PAPERS AND REPORTS

The difference between academic and nonacademic reports is that the latter are less theoretically driven. The world outside of academics is a more concrete place. People are much more likely to believe in "simple facts." Usually, the reason that nonacademic research is undertaken is because someone wants to know what the "simple facts" are.

This means that you have to know pretty much everything that goes into the academic report, but you do not need to tell anyone. Unless they ask, of course, and you will be surprised at the level of conceptual sophistication you can run into in a group of "average people."

A nonacademic report is stripped down so that you can get to the data faster. The data themselves are much more important in nonacademic than in academic reports. An academic report is an intricate weave of your ideas, the ideas of others, data, analysis, and interpretation. A nonacademic report is almost pure methodology—almost entirely empirical. The goal is not to further ideas but to gain information.

Because of this change in emphasis, a nonacademic report consists of the following:

1. Statement of a charge
2. Operationalizations of key terms
3. Research design
4. Sampling
5. Analysis
6. Interpretations, conclusions, recommendations

Statement of a Charge

In group discussion courses, decision-making groups are said to have a "charge." A charge is a statement of a group's purpose. The charge contains very precise statements concerning the problem with which the group is faced, the type of product the group must produce, the time line, and so on. In a nonacademic research report, the charge replaces the theory and review of the literature sections.

The introductory paragraph of *Strategic Directions: A Needs Assessment and Industry Targeting Analysis of Stanislaus County* (Entin, Aly, Sumser, & Giventer, 1997) says:

> As a new century approaches and a new state economy emerges, it is an opportune time to ask a number of searching economic development questions: Is Stanislaus County fully prepared and well-positioned to participate constructively in the future economy? Does Stanislaus County have distinguishing competitive assets and resources that will enable it to make a special contribution? What are the county's competitive assets and liabilities linked to economic development? What are the opportunities and threats? Who are the competitors in economic development and how does this area match up against them? Are there distinctive and preferred targets of economic development that can or should be pursued? If these avenues are pursued, what must be done to neutralize threats and convert weaknesses into strengths?
>
> These are the questions addressed in this report. (p. 1)

Note that we are careful to say that the questions are *addressed,* not *answered.* This paragraph tells the reader what guided us. There are numerous theories of economic development, but they are not discussed. There are thousands of articles about economic development, but they are not cited.

Operationalizations of Key Terms

Operationalization should be kept to a minimum. Its purpose, as always, is to clarify what you mean by key terms. With applied research, it is often best to find out what the client means by certain terms or what certain terms mean within the target industry.

It is a good idea to sit down with representatives of your target audience to clarify your charge and to go over key operationalizations in your design. When, in academic research, you do a literature review, you are making sure that the way you are thinking about a problem is in line with the way the problem is conceptualized by others in the field. Often in applied research this is not possible. Because of this, a meeting with representatives of your target audience to go over your charge and key concepts serves the same function as a review of the literature.

Once you have had a meeting to review these things, you will have a good sense of which concepts will have to be articulated in the actual report. If there is a standard operationalization within the target industry, there will be no need to spell out operationalizations in the report itself.

Research Design

The methodological section of the *Strategic Directions* report quoted above is tucked away on the inside front cover with the heading "A Note on Data." It is not an integral part of the text.

The report does not build an argument about ideas. It builds a descriptive answer to pragmatic questions. The questions themselves, you will notice, are not necessarily nontheoretical. They are *treated* as nontheoretical only because this is a nonacademic report.

Generally, any audience for a nonacademic report is going to be divided. The reason information is perceived as needed is that more than one course of action is plausible and more than one course of action has proponents. Inevitable, the research will favor one side or the other, and the side that "loses" will want to

> **SIDEBAR 5.9 Formal Style Tip**
>
> A *sidebar* is a separate section that contains additional information but that need not be read for the main flow of the text to be understood.
>   The Formal Style Tips in this chapter are sidebars.

check your methodology. Your research design and sample must be included, in however brief a form, somewhere in the report. Do not build it into the report itself because it will disrupt the narrative flow. In nonacademic reports, the methodology sections are best relegated to an appendix—or something resembling an appendix or a "sidebar."

Sampling

Sampling should go with the rest of the research design. This does not have to be tremendously detailed. If any odd sampling decisions had to be made, you should be ready to articulate and justify them if the occasion arises.

Analysis

Analysis in applied research is determined by the standards of the audience. Some audiences for applied research are very sophisticated. If you are writing a program evaluation for social service workers, for example, you can use fairly sophisticated statistical analyses. The same is quite often true when you do applied research for health care workers or for marketing people. For most people in business or politics, however, you should only use percentage differences, raw numbers, and two-by-two tables.

Interpretation, Conclusions, Recommendations

In nonacademic research, it is a good idea to summarize your findings in a series of bullet points. Do not overinterpret the data. Most people receiving nonacademic research results are not looking for nuanced findings. The questions are blunt: Does it work? Will they come? Who are these people? Are we gaining market share or losing market share?

Conclusions and recommendations should also be summarized in bullet points.

A written nonacademic report is very similar to a face-to-face presentation.

SUMMARY

A friend recently asked if I could summarize my idea of a research methods course in one sentence. I told her it was a course in how to be clear. If she had given me a few more sentences, I would have said that it is a course in how to ask clear, answerable questions. It is a course in how to figure out and articulate the way one goes about answering those questions. Finally, it is a course in how to communicate the whole research process to others.

To summarize the chapter on writing, then, the message is that you must write clearly. To write clearly, you must know who your audience is. This is especially important in nonacademic research. In academic research, you know who your audience is and how they think because your audience consists of all the people who wrote the articles and books that you reviewed.

ACTIVITIES AND EXERCISES

1. Find an article in a major communication journal and outline it.
2. Get a paper you wrote last semester and outline it.

NOTE

1. Note that you can have a philosophical *theory* but that you have religious *beliefs*. This is because a philosophical theory is testable, just not testable empirically. It must pass tests at the logical level. This is not true of religious beliefs, which can quite comfortably contain blank spots and contradictions. It is not possible to refute a religious belief logically anymore than it is possible to refute it empirically. This means that religious beliefs are not theories.

PART II

THE APPLICATIONS

6

FIELDWORK:

Looking at People in Actual Environments

The best way to see how people behave is to watch them. In the introduction to this book, we said we would look at four ways to gather data: fieldwork, experiments, surveys, and content analysis. Of these, only fieldwork allows us to see people behaving in normal situations. Although we will discuss some exceptions to this, *experiments* generally look at people's behavior under laboratory conditions, which, as Neil Postman (1993) noted, are not conditions in which most people spend very much time. *Surveys* ask people to describe their behavior or beliefs, and *content analysis* for the most part looks at mass media products such as television programs, advertisements, and newspaper editorials.

Field research allows us to watch people in natural settings and to engage them in conversation, asking them to explain what it is they are doing. One of the reasons that fieldwork is so valuable to communication scholars is that it is as much about that how people talk as it is about descriptions of their activities. In much of field research, the goal is to understand what that people are doing *from their perspectives*. This makes fieldwork as much a study of conceptualization as observation.

In this chapter, we will look at fieldwork ranging from pure observation through field experimentation. The sidebars in this chapter are designed to show you two things about field research. First, they show how data are presented and arguments made within the context of field research. Pay particular attention to how descriptions and interpretations are continuously interwoven. The sidebars will be discussed in the section called "Writing." Second, the sidebars show you the different levels of involvement required of the field researcher. You will see that the field researcher is involved, to various degrees, in what is being studied. The social and intellectual distance required of more rigidly scientific methods is not present here.

QUESTIONS OF VALIDITY AND RELIABILITY

Because fieldwork allows us to actually see people as they act in real life, it has very high *validity.* Validity means that the way you gather information is relevant to real life. Because you gathered your data in real life, it is obviously relevant.

Imagine that you are interested in finding out how courteous people are and you have to decide which method to use. In an experiment, you could set up an artificial situation in which people have the opportunity either to be or not to be polite. In a survey, you could ask people how courteous they are in various situations. The problem with the experiment is that it is artificial, and the problem with the survey is that we have no idea how polite people are, only how polite they *say* they are. Because of this, these ways of collecting information run the risk of having low validity. Only fieldwork lets you find out how courteous people actually are in real situations.

One of the problems with fieldwork is that it is relatively *unscientific.* This is because scientific research is based on control and the ability to repeat the research. *Control,* in science, means the ability to limit the sort of complexity that affects every real-life situation. In fieldwork, the researcher watches people in normal

SIDEBAR 6.1 In Practice: Interviews in Real Life

People wonder why researchers just don't *ask* people to tell us about themselves instead of conducting experiments or doing field research. The following interview with Jeff, a 14-year-old boy, shows how difficult it is to apply the conceptual frameworks used in research in a straightforward interview:

Interviewer: Please tell me about yourself by completing this sentence: "I am a _____."

Jeff: I ain't no good at this.

I: [laugh] You're not any good at this? [pause] Okay, if I say to you, "I am a blank," what pops into your mind?

J: [pause] A nice young boy.

I: Great. That's just what we're looking for. . . . [After giving more examples of possible answers and getting no- where, we moved to another subject] . . . [pause] Well, how about thinking about yourself in relationships with other people? . . . What role do you think of then?

J: I don't understand.

I: Well, we could talk about family roles. Do you have a role . . . in your family? [pause] How about you're Mrs. [Brown's] son? That's a role.

J: Oh.

I: Does that make sense?

J: Yeah, I guess.

I: Do you have any relationships with anyone else? [10-second pause while Jeff thinks] How about friends?

J: Yeah.

I: Whose friend are you?

J: Todd's.

Each of the six teens in this phase of the research was confused and somewhat embarrassed when confronted with the words *role* and *identity*. Despite an ongoing at-tempt to come up with alternative ways of getting at these concepts, we never found substitute words that worked well. What we did notice, however, was that when we talked with teens in their bedrooms we were surrounded by visual clues as to who these young people were and what they valued. (Brown, Dykers, Steele, & White, 1994, pp. 821-822) situations and has very little control. Unlike a tightly controlled experiment or a survey in which it is always possible to ask exactly the same questions of additional people, a field research project can never be precisely controlled or repeated. The ability to repeat research is known as *replication* (a combination of "repetition" and "duplication") and is very important because it allows us to test previous research to see if the results were reliable and not simply a fluke of circumstances. The ability to be replicated is known as *reliability*. The results are *reliable* if they can be replicated and shown not to be a matter of chance.

So you can see that because fieldwork occurs in real life it has very high *validity* but very low *reliability*. As you will see in this volumn, there is a tension between validity and reliability. Increases in validity usually result in decreases in reliability. The opposite is also true: Increases in reliability usually result in decreases in validity. It is also important to keep in mind that validity is the more important of the two concepts. It was stressed in the chapter on operationalization that it is more important that the concept make sense (validity) than that the concept be measurable (reliability). Think of Postman's (1993) example of female beauty discussed in the chapter on conceptualization.

All research involves a tug of war between reliability and validity. In all research, if it is to be properly called research and not opinion or fiction or propaganda, some attention must be paid to both concepts. This tension between validity and reliability can be seen in the two main types of fieldwork. The least intrusive is *ethnography*, in which the researcher does not attempt to manipulate the situation being examined. Sometimes researchers take a more aggressive role and manipulate the environment or situation in such a way that the research becomes a blend of fieldwork and experimentation that is called a *field experiment* or a *quasi-experiment*. We will look at each of these in turn.

ETHNOGRAPHY

Ethnography is a research method developed by anthropologists to explore exotic cultures. Its application expanded as the

SIDEBAR 6.2 Excerpt From *America's Working Man,* by David Halle (1984, p. 62)

But for most workers . . . school was a period when their self-esteem was under continual attack.

How did they cope with this? Some simply accepted the school's assessment of their intellect. As one, in his late forties, explained:

> I was a real dummy. When I was in school if we got a question right we moved forward a chair in class and if we got a question wrong we moved back a chair. I was always at the back.

More commonly men distance themselves from the school's judgement. Sometimes they accept personal responsibility for academic failure but explain that the problem was they did not work hard enough: "I was lazy at school," "I fucked up," I didn't study," "I wasn't interested," "I should have worked harder." Such explanations, true or false, are clearly easier for a man to accept than is the idea that his intellect is inferior.

But the most frequent way men account for their failure in school is by blaming the curriculum and the teachers. The curriculum was irrelevant and the teachers were inept, malevolent, or exploitative. Consider the following, from a worker in his late forties, a mechanic:

> What was school like? It was horrible, horrible! Those teachers, they didn't care. One said to me, "You're going to end up in a factory anyway, what are you wasting your time here for?"
>
> They [the teachers] were cuckoos. They gave you Romeo and Juliet to read, and I looked at it and I said, "What is this! What has this got to do with me?" I looked on the flyleaf. You know, back then they passed books down from one class to the next, so you could see who'd had your book two or three years ago. And I saw Joe Smith's name from three years ago. I knew he was digging ditches now, so I said to myself, "This book didn't do anything for him. What's it going to do for me?"

SIDEBAR 6.3 Excerpt From *Working Knowledge:*
**   *Skill and Community in a Small Shop,***
**   by Douglas Harper (1987, pp. 117-118)**

[This is a study of the workshop of an old-fashioned mechanic named Willie. In the excerpt below, Harper begins by discussing one of his ideas about work, an idea developed from watching Willie, then quotes the novelist Robert Pirsig, author of *Zen and the Art of Motorcycle Maintenance*, then provides a number of illustrations of his point in Willie's own words. Harper's ability to integrate ideas and observation makes this one of the best qualitative studies I have read.]

There is a kinesthetic correctness to Willie's method. This in and of itself makes his mechanicking different from that of the "parts changer," the formally trained by-the-book professional that I have referred to as the rationalized repairman. . . . But it is difficult to learn how hard to hit or twist a tool, or how to interpret the sound of a running machine from written instructions. Often when you observe a mechanic who works only "by the book," you see that he is unable to use his body efficiently. Thus either materials are not used to their limits and the job gets stuck or they are pushed beyond their limits and parts are broken. Willie's working method builds on a detailed knowledge of materials and develops precisely the kind of tactile, empirical connection that leads to smooth working rhythms, appropriate power and torque, and the interpretation of sounds and subtle physical sensations. Robert Pirsig describes this quality of work:

There's what's called a "mechanic's feel," which is very obvious to those who know what it is, but hard to describe to those who don't. . . . The mechanic's feel comes from a deep inner kinesthetic feeling for the elasticity of materials. Some materials, like ceramics, have little; . . . other materials, like steel, have tremendous elasticity, more than rubber.

> Although I have chosen a number of examples to illustrate
> these ideas, all presentations of Willie's work in this book
> reflect to some degree the theme of the unity of work, the
> marriage of the hand and mind, in solving practical
> problems.
>
> . . . Yeah [says Willie], it looks like I am holding the file
> real tender like [in the photograph]. But you've got to shift
> that pressure from one hand to another—as you go
> across the saw the pressure shifts on your file. If you hold
> it hard, you can't feel the pressure. You're not gripping
> the file, you're more or less letting it float or glide right
> through.

interests of anthropologists expanded and as researchers in other disciplines adopted it. Rather than looking only at exotic cultures (i.e., cultures much different than one's own), an ethnographer can look at any cultural or subcultural activity to gain an understanding of how it works, what it means, or why it takes the form that it does.

The key element of the ethnographic method is that it is nonintrusive. This does not mean that it is not intrusive at all: Whenever human life is studied, what is being studied is affected by the presence of the researcher, and what the researcher sees is affected by the conceptual framework that is being used to understand what is going on. What it means is that, to the extent that it is possible, the researcher tries not to interfere, manipulate, or alter the situation, activities, or environment that is being studied.

This is not always easy. As an outsider, the researcher has to fit into the environment in some way, and the way one fits in is not always a matter of the researcher's preference. The roles that can be played by the researcher range from being a pure observer to being a participant who observes. Quite often, unless one participates in some fashion it is not possible to get access to the information and experiences in which one is interested. Studies of

**SIDEBAR 6.4 Excerpt From *Amana:
From Pietist Sect to American Community*,
by Diane L. Barthel (1984, p. xiv)**

I myself came to Amana somewhat as a pilgrim. My mother
had grown up there and left before the Change. As a girl, I
visited the colonies several times and listened to stories of
the old Amana. Coming back to conduct historical and field
research in the summers of 1977-79, I found my entree
eased both by members of my extended family residing there
and by the cooperation and assistance of individuals associated with the Museum of Amana History, the Amana Society,
and the Amana Church Society. I undertook participant
observation and also conducted both formal and informal
interviews covering all aspects of community life and organization. Formal interviews were usually conducted at work,
informal interviews at home. Out of respect for my informants and a desire to protect their anonymity, I have
avoided identifying the sources of quotations in the text and
have sometimes changed the identity of the village following
a quotation.

. . . This book thus exists at the intersection of the personal and the theoretical. It is an interpretive history, one
that uses Amana's historical course to raise questions that
individuals and communities across the nation face as they
come to terms with their individual and collective pasts.

restaurant life, for example, have been conducted by researchers
employed as cocktail waitresses. These researchers argued that it
wasn't possible to get an understanding of the kinds of interactions experienced by cocktail waitresses just by watching them at
work.

Studying deviant groups tends to require that one participate.
It would be interesting, for example, to get an understanding of
the way skinheads and neo-Nazis explain their experiences, but it
is unlikely that such groups would allow a neutral researcher in as

> **SIDEBAR 6.5 Excerpt From *The Spirit Catches You and You Fall Down: A Hmong Child, Her American Doctors, and the Collision of Two Cultures*, by Anne Fadiman (1997, pp. 140-141)**
>
> "When the spirit caught Lia and she fell down," said Nao Kao, "she was usually sick for ten minutes or so. After that, she would be normal again, and if you gave her rice, she ate it. But this time she was really sick for a long time, so we had to call our nephew because he spoke English and he knew how to call an ambulance." On every other occasion when Lia had seized, Nao Kao and Foua had carried Lia to the hospital. I asked Nao Kao why he had decided to summon an ambulance. "If you take her in an ambulance, they would pay more attention to her at the hospital," he said. "If you don't call the ambulance, those tsov tom people wouldn't look at her." May Ying hesitated before translating tsov tom, which means "tiger bite." Tigers are a symbol of wickedness and duplicity—in Hmong folktales, they steal men's wives and eat their own children—and tsov tom is a very serious curse.

a pure observer. At the very least, it seems that the researcher would have to show some sympathy, tolerance, or understanding of the group's position to be allowed access. Of course, the researcher could always access such groups by going "undercover" and becoming a participant-observer, but not only is that dangerous, it also raises ethical problems about deception.

THE QUESTIONS

Different types of questions are best answered using different types of research methods. A researcher named Nick Trujillo (1992) was interested in the culture of baseball. He wanted to learn what the game means to the people who spend their lives working in the ballparks. To get at this, Trujillo used field research methods. The data he reported in his study "were collected using participant observation and interview methods and were gathered over a period of two years" (p. 352). Trujillo spent a great deal of time wandering around the ballpark and talking with the people who worked there and with the fans. As a fan sitting up in the stands, he was a participant-observer because he acted pretty much like all the other fans.

Among the employees, he was much more a pure observer. He turned down the opportunity, for example, to try out different jobs such as food vendor, usher, or security guard in favor of his role as observer. To understand more about the employees, he "attended pre-season orientations for security guards, food vendors, Stadium Club waitresses, ushers, ticket tellers, and parking lot attendants to see how ballpark managers trained their employees" (p. 353). He was a participant observer when he studied the fans because he was a fan when he did so, but because he learned about the workers only by watching them and talking to them he was a pure observer when he studied them.

You can see that the kinds of questions that field researchers have are loosely focused. The questions concern how things work or feel in actual life. Other questions concern the meaning attributed to things or activities by those who experience them on a daily basis. Baseball, for example, may mean nothing to you, but it may mean a great deal to the fans, players, owners, ballpark staff, and reporters who spend their lives in and around the game. And the meaning that field researchers are looking for is not the public-relations-handout or the what-would-they-say-if-you-asked type of meaning, but meaning in the sense of how baseball fits into actual lives and how people talk about it among themselves, value it, and treat it.

Baseball is a subculture, but everyone is part of some subculture, and subcultures contain what Clifford Geertz (1973) called "local knowledge," what Polanyi (1962) called "hand knowledge," and what Wittgenstein (1968) called "knowing how to go on" (p. 60). All these forms of knowledge are normative. They are not written down and are a blend of art, technique, and local tradition. They may not even be capable of being articulated by the people who possess the knowledge, and because of this, the only way for an outsider to gain the knowledge is to become, to some degree, part of the scene.

There are many outstanding examples of fieldwork, most of which, you'll notice, are in book rather than article format. Why this is the case will become obvious in the section of this chapter entitled "Data." A suggestive list of the kinds of fieldwork related to communication that people have done recently includes Donna Gaines's *Teenage Wasteland* (1998), a study of alienated teenagers in New Jersey; Jerry Halle's *America's Working Man* (1984), a study of how blue-collar workers think about work and what it means to them; Douglas Harper's *Working Knowledge* (1987), a study of the knowledge in a small handyman's shop in rural Vermont; and Mitchell Duneier's *Sidewalk* (1999), an examination of the social worlds of street vendors in New York City.

FIELD EXPERIMENTS

One of the problems with fieldwork is that if you have a narrowly focused question it may be hard to collect data. Let's imagine that you are interested in how strangers use different conversational strategies to get to know one another. You could sit on a street corner or in a tavern and wait for the proper sort of interactions to occur—but that could mean a tremendous amount of time wasted while nothing happened. Or you could become more active, more manipulative, and create the situations you were interested in studying: You could go to a lot of parties, social gatherings, or singles bars and approach strangers to see how they reacted and the strategies they used in defining your relationship.

By manipulating the situation, you introduce variables into it. Variables, as pointed out in Chapter 2, are used to simplify and standardize situations. An excellent example of this can be found in Sobel and Lillith's (1975) study of personal space, an aspect of nonverbal communication. Most studies of personal space involved fairly static situations such as conversational distances or seating arrangements. But Sobel and Lillith wanted to know how the idea of personal space worked itself out among pedestrians on the sidewalks of New York City.

One way of studying the idea of personal space among pedestrians would be to sit near the sidewalk and observe the patterns created by those people walking past. When do people slow down or speed up to create distance? How is passing accomplished? What do you do about oncoming pedestrian traffic? The problem with doing this is that there is so much happening on a busy sidewalk that your impressions as an observer would be hard to relate to the static-distance studies (mentioned above), which were very precise in terms of measured distances. Because they wanted to conduct research that could be related to the earlier research, Sobel and Lillith decided that they needed more control than they could get using ethnographic methods.

Sobel and Lillith created research teams consisting of one "pedestrian" and two observers. The stretch of sidewalk to be observed was marked so that distances could be calculated rather than simply estimated, and then the "pedestrian" member of the team walked directly toward an oncoming pedestrian to see how, and when, the real pedestrian would react.

This is an example of a field experiment. Unlike the ethnographic study of the baseball stadium, in which the researcher had no control over the situation being observed, this sidewalk study gave the researchers a great deal of control. Obviously, they could not control the reaction of the real pedestrians, but that was the object of the study, so controlling it would make no sense. What they could, and did, control was the way in which personal space was threatened and the sex of both the invading "pedestrian" and the target pedestrian.

This is a field experiment because it happened in a real place in real life rather than in a laboratory. Field experiments are sometimes called "pseudo-experiments" because it is not possible to control all the variables. Ideally, everything except the reaction of the pedestrian should be under control, but in this experiment all sorts of things were out of the researcher's control. Traffic noises and movement, the movement of other pedestrians, and familiarity of the target pedestrian with the neighborhood are all things that could influence the way the target pedestrian would react, and all of these were out of the researcher's control.

Still, in this study, unlike the baseball study, it was possible to say, "Let's do it four more times and then call it day" or "Let's try the same thing in Cincinnati." The study could be *replicated.* It could be replicated because the researchers had a great deal of control. Field experiments are an attempt to blend the validity of fieldwork with the reliability of experimentation. Because of this, field experiments can be quite persuasive.

Not only can fieldwork be considered along a range from ethnography to field experiments, but field experiments can range from being mildly aggressive manipulations to fairly rigidly structured experiments such as Sobel and Lillith's sidewalk intervention discussed above. A student doing a field study of the sexual harassment of cocktail waitresses, for example, modified her interaction style with customers to see if it had any impact on harassment. She would alter her behavior from very formal-professional to friendly to bantering and make note of the quality of customer interaction that went along with each style. This approach is mildly manipulative compared with the very formal experimental structure used in the street intervention.

VARIABLES AND CONCEPTUALIZATIONS

When field experiments become rigidly formalized, as was the case in the sidewalk study, then the use of variables and conceptualizations is similar to what will be discussed in Chapter 7 on experiments. This chapter will focus on looser field experiments and on ethnography.

Ideally, fieldwork is used to generate, rather than test, conceptualizations. For this reason, fieldwork is associated with *grounded theory,* which is the effort to base theories on empirical observations. Basically, grounded theorists want to look before they think. They claim that the problem with too many theorists is that they think before they look, if they bother looking at all. Because of this approach, fieldwork conceptualization consists of organizing one's impressions and ideas as one conducts research and as one writes up the results.

This method of conceptualization is known as the *hermeneutic circle.* The circularity comes from the constant evolution of concepts as one looks, then thinks, then looks, then thinks. In practice, this means that you approach the situation to be studied without a preconceived conceptual framework. "Preconceived conceptual framework" is a fancy way of saying that you walk into a situation thinking you know what is going on before you ever get there and then jam your experience into the pigeonholes your ideas have created and dismiss any information that doesn't fit as irrelevant.

Instead, in grounded theory, you let the ideas rise out of the experience and then use the ideas to help focus your experience. It is as Kant said: You need experience to get ideas, and then you use your ideas to get an understanding of your experience. When I was in the Peace Corps in Afghanistan, the bus going out to my village would always stop at one point, just before the road wound up a small hill and then descended between low cliffs to the plain beyond. When it stopped, the passengers would all make a gesture that looked very much as if they were washing their faces. Curious about this, I asked a man in my village what it meant, and he told me that Afghans did not make such gestures. Later, I asked some people in the country's capital and was told the same thing.

I knew that ritual washing is an important part of Islam and that Afghanistan is an Islamic nation. Because of this, I suspected that the washing gesture was based in religion, whether or not this was the connection made by the people themselves. With this in mind, I began to watch for the gesture on my various bus trips. The washing gesture was not made very often, but when it was, it was made at the beginning of trips and at dangerous areas such as the entry to the Kabul Gorge, a narrow, treacherous road that plunges down the mountains dividing the northern and southern parts of the country. I asked around and found that the place outside my village where the bus always stopped had been the scene of a grisly accident in which a busload of people had been killed when one of the cliffs had collapsed in an earthquake.

Usually, ethnographic research is more complex than this example illustrates, but it still serves as a good example of how I made sense of the gesture I had seen on the bus. First, I noticed the gesture. The key to ethnography is the ability to notice things, to see patterns and connections, and odd unexpected little things. The old expression, "God is in the details" could be adapted to ethnography to read that culture (and meaning) is in the little things that form the tapestry of unremarkable assumptions of everyday life.

With religion as a framework, the fact that the gesture was made at the beginning of journeys and at dangerous locales made sense. We tend to seek the help of spiritual beings at the transition points of our lives. If the gesture had been made more or less randomly, then the religious connection would not have been so useful. Then, with the religious idea and the observation that the gesture was made at specific times and places, I asked about the locale where I first saw the gesture made and found that it was perceived as a dangerous place in which many local residents had died. And that completed the circle: I then understood why the bus stopped and the gesture was made. I knew what it meant, at least to the extent that I now knew when the gesture was appropriate.

My understanding of Islam had helped me understand a particular practice, and my understanding of that practice gave me a better understanding of Islam. This sort of circularity prevents the operationalization discussed in Chapter 3 in which a variable is operationalized *prior* to looking at the world. Instead of approaching the world with clear, testable concepts, the ethnographer is much more comfortable with a bit of murkiness and flexibility. One could say that the ethnographer seeks understanding rather than knowledge and that because the actors in the situation do not have clearly articulated concepts the researcher does not need them either. There is, I would think, something to this, but the idea that knowledge and understanding are completely different things is a little odd and more than a little artificial—like something said in a philosophy class.

SAMPLING

Usually when we talk of sampling in the social sciences, we mean the selection of people from whom we are going to get information: whom we send the questionnaires to, whom we poll on the telephone, whom we recruit to participate in the experiments. In fieldwork, we sample not only people but places and times.

In the ballpark study, Trujillo did not try to speak to everyone so much as he tried to cover all the different aspects of the park. To be able to describe the baseball culture, he had to look at not only the players and owners but the park managers, hotdog salesmen, ticket takers, groundskeepers, sportscasters, waitresses, and fans. His *sample design* had to include all these people.

Sampling of people is not very formal in fieldwork. You just have to make sure that you look at all the people you need to understand what is going on. The hermeneutic circle approach suggests that at first you study pretty much everyone and then focus on select people as you learn more. When studying communication flows in an organization, for example, at first you look at everyone, but then you may notice that there are "old guard" and "newcomer" groupings and that the key to the communication flow seems be to located in the interaction between these two organizational subcultures. You want to make sure that you don't end up taking the point of view of only one of the groups.

In the sidewalk study, people were not sampled at all. Instead, parts of town and times of day were selected because there is no uniform city culture; instead, there is a collection of smaller neighborhood cultures that change with the time of day and the day of the week. The financial and political centers of a major city might be a key element of its culture, for example, but these areas should not be studied on Saturday afternoon because the people (and the cultural emphasis) have shifted to more domestic and entertainment concerns.

A similar consideration is necessary when studying organizations. Mondays may not be the same as Wednesdays, and morning may not be the same as midafternoon. Location could also be a major consideration: how close one is to corporate headquarters, how large one's department is, and what floor one is on could all be meaningful in the corporate culture.

There is a scene in the movie *My Dinner with André* in which one of the two characters says that he wants to deal with people as individuals and ignore all the artificial social divisions, but while he is saying this he is absolutely ignoring the waiter who is serving them. In all organizations, there are equally invisible people who are crucial to the functioning of the organization, and these people should be included in your sampling design. There are also marginal people in every organization, and a great deal can be learned by studying the unpopular and alienated people in any group. Why they *don't* fit tells you why some people *do* fit, and this tells you a lot about how the group maintains itself.

The key to sampling in fieldwork is being systematic and really thinking about what you want to talk about. Sampling charts should be drawn up so that you can make sure you are covering all your bases. Plan whom you want to talk with or observe, and plan what and when you want to observe, and even within the fluid methodology of fieldwork you should be able to cover all the ground you wanted to cover. There is nothing more frustrating than seeing gaps in your fieldwork when you are writing up your report 6 months later and it is impossible to go back to get more information.

One sampling technique that can be used in fieldwork is called *snowball sampling.* In a snowball sample, you ask each person you speak to if he or she knows of someone else you might be able to talk to. This works best if your fieldwork relies more heavily on interviews than on observations. Its primary weakness is that you may end up avoiding marginal people (because no one will refer you to them). This will create a bias in your sample.

DATA COLLECTION AND ANALYSIS

Data collection and analysis basically come in two forms: *qualitative* and *quantitative.* The difference between them is that qualitative analysis does not reduce information to numerical scores whereas quantitative research does. In fieldwork—with the exception of formal field experiments—the data are not numeric, so the research is *qualitative.* This distinction between qualitative and quantitative research corresponds to the distinction between ideographic and nomothetic research that was discussed in Chapter 2.

In practice, qualitative analysis means that you introduce your data to the reader in words rather than numbers. In other words, what persuades the reader that your research is accurate or insightful is not the square root of some objectively obtained number but your ability to write lucid, logical, convincing prose. For this reason, most qualitative work is done in book rather than article form. Numbers are reductionist in that numerals and formulas are allowed to stand in for very complex realities. Qualitative work is *thick*—the opposite of reductionist—so what reductionists can reduce to a single graph can take tens, if not hundreds, of pages in a qualitative form. Of course, the reduction of those hundreds of pages to a single graph involves an immense loss of information and is part of the validity-reliability trade-off that researchers make.

Data collection is usually done as unobtrusively as possible. It is best that observations be recorded off scene or after your day's research has been completed. Data can be recorded in small note-books, tape recorders, or (somewhat more intrusively) laptop computers.

The data of ethnographic work constitute what is called a "thick description." The description is *thick* in that it contains as much information as possible. This is for two reasons. First, be-cause of the hermeneutic approach, you have no idea what may turn out to be important. So you need to write down as much as possible. Second, regardless of what you may think, your mem-ory is a sieve—worse than a sieve, in fact, because it not only leaks, it leaks selectively and distorts what it doesn't lose. Write down every bit of information, every impression, and every name, time, and place that you can as soon as you can.

All of these notes should be entered into a log of some sort as soon as you get back to your office or home. Ideally, the log should be a word-processing file in a computer because this allows you to search later for key words and sort information. Entering your notes into a larger file allows you to expand them, to make notes to yourself, and to add as much detail as possible.

Qualitative analysis is very difficult. It requires not only a tre-mendous eye for nuances but also superior writing skills to orga-nize your notes into a coherent narrative. If you do not like to write (and rewrite), then you should not do fieldwork.

WRITING

When writing any research paper, it is important that the reader know exactly what you have done. In a fieldwork paper, this re-quires that the reader know how you obtained access, what you did once you obtained access, and what you saw and are now us-ing as data. It is very important that the reader get a feel for the environment you are describing. What is convincing in a field-work report is the sense of authenticity—the author conveying to the reader the sense that he or she has actually been there and has understood what was going on.

Let's look at the examples of writing that were included in this chapter in the sidebars.

In Sidebar 6.2 on page 105, David Halle (1984) uses quotes from his subjects to make his points. In this section, Halle sets up the question in the first paragraph and then gives a series of illustrations of the different ways the men interviewed described their time in school. In the two middle paragraphs, Halle describes two main strategies—distancing and blaming the curriculum—and then continues with quotations. This is a great example of how you can let people speak for themselves and yet organize their comments into a cohesive narrative. You can see that if he simply told you that men "most commonly . . . distance themselves from the school's judgment" you would get very little sense of how the men reconciled themselves with their educational pasts. He gives you the words the men used, and you can see both how the men thought about their pasts and what Halle means by "distancing."

Sidebar 6.3 on page 106 is an excerpt from Douglas Harper's *Working Knowledge* (1987), one of my favorite fieldwork studies. Harper observes the way Willie works—that is the central thrust of the book—but to make sense of his observations, Harper integrates remarks made by novelist Robert Pirsig, comments made by Willie, and his own judgments. Field research needs this sort of integrated approach. The goal is to understand the situations and lives lived by other people, so the field researcher pulls from observation—what can actually be *seen*—and marries it to what the subjects say, what different thinkers have said about similar things, and what the researcher thinks is going on, based on personal experience. The sidebar excerpting Fadiman (1997) also shows us how you can merge quotes, descriptions, and explanations to make sense of an event. Both Harper and Fadiman, like many field researchers, are trying to present a form of life to people who are unfamiliar with it, and because of this, "pure descriptions" are not enough.

Fieldwork is a merging of the personal and the objective, the intellectual and the experiential. In Sidebar 6.4 on page 108, Diane Barthel (1984), the researcher, tells us how she is connected to the community she studied and how she went about studying it. She tells us that the work "exists at the intersection of the personal and the theoretical" (p. xiv). I think all good fieldwork takes place at that intersection. Certainly, Donna Gaines's (1998) study of alienated suburban teens merges the personal and the theoretical, as does Mitchell Duneier's (1999) wonderful look at street vendors in New York City. When writing fieldwork, you should not pretend otherwise. The author is always part of the description because the author's perspective is always obvious. The author is also always part of the argument: The credibility of the research is tied very strongly to the perception of the author's credibility.

This means, in practical terms, that you can use the first-person pronoun usually forbidden in academic research. It means that you can tell us how you found out about certain things, even if you found out by pure chance, because in fieldwork, as in life, being able to recognize a chance opportunity is a rare and respected quality.

COMMENTS

Ethical Issues

Fieldwork is based on a great deal of trust. Betraying that trust is the biggest issue facing a field researcher. Duneier (*Sidewalk*) has the permission of all the main characters he discusses in his book. Most of these people have read what Duneier has written about them, and one of the key figures in his study has written the afterword in the book. This goes beyond what is required by professional ethics, but it shows how much Duneier respects his subjects. Respect for the rights of your subjects is the key to almost all ethical concerns in research methods.

Duneier's subjects knew that he was writing a book about them. In all the studies discussed in this chapter, the subjects knew they were being studied. This may not always be the case. I met a woman who was writing a book about women in the militia movement. This researcher had decided not to tell her subjects what it was she was doing. She was afraid that if she told the members of the militia that she was an academic, she would be denied access. The decision concerning whether you tell your subjects is one that needs to be carefully considered. A decision *not* to tell your subjects is one that needs to be reviewed by colleagues. In universities, there are usually formal committees for such reviews. The basic position in the social sciences is that research subjects should be informed and must be protected.

You should also be aware that researchers do not have the protection of the *shield laws* that are designed to protect journalists. Field researchers quite often can observe behavior that is illegal. You do not have a right to keep your sources anonymous.

Concealing the identity (and often the locale) of your subjects is the norm. The sort of research communication scholars are involved in is usually designed to be generalizable to larger groups or applicable to broader questions, and because of this, the precise identity of your subjects or informants is not crucial. The convention is that you simply make up new names when names are necessary in the stories you tell.

Connections

Field research, as you have seen, shades off into experimental research. There is not a hard and fast delineation between the two; rather, there is a continuum. The two methods, however, have very different *logics,* so you have to be clear about which dominates the research you are doing. In pure, qualitative fieldwork, you are less theory driven, more exploratory. In field experiments, you are more likely to be testing hypotheses and quantifying your data. Because of the manipulation, if you are engaging in field experiments, then you should make sure you follow the ethical guidelines for experiments, which are more rigid than those for fieldwork.

SIDEBAR 6.6 **Vocabulary**		
Ethnography	Field experiment	Grounded theory
Qualitative data	Quantitative data	Quasi-experiment
Reductionist	Replication	Thick description

Quite often in fieldwork, you are not simply reporting behavior. You are also interested in reporting how the subjects think about (and talk about) their lives and experiences. When you are trying to reduce a large number of comments and conversations into usable data, you are engaging in *content analysis*, which is discussed later in this book.

ACTIVITIES AND EXERCISES

1. Read *Close Encounters* by John Sumser (1986) (Appendix B). What sort of observer was he? What sort of sampling did he do? What sort of sampling do you think he should have done?
2. In the cafeteria, there are long tables that are usually shared by strangers or groups of strangers. Observe two of these tables for a half hour and write up your observations. How do these individuals or groups interact with each other? Is the communication primarily verbal or nonverbal? What conclusion, if any, can you draw about these people?

7

THE EXPERIMENT

Walter Lippmann (1922) said that the "booming, buzzing confusion" of life had to be tamed by language in order to be understood. The complexity and idiosyncrasies of life would overwhelm us if we tried to deal only with life's uniqueness, so we organize the world into patterns and categories that standardize. the world to the point where we can begin to grasp it. The fieldwork method, as you have seen, tries to "tame" life as little as possible in the search for understanding, but the fieldworker pays a price for this. The field research approach to the world is fairly passive, the questions lack precision, the information is difficult to manage, and the answers are open to interpretation.

The experiment, in contrast, is the tool of science. Centuries ago, Sir Francis Bacon, one of the founders of modern science, saw the experiment as a way to "put nature to the test" (quoted in Leis, 1972, p. 57). And the test he had in mind was the rack, that device designed to stretch the truth out of human prisoners. Nothing wishy-washy about this. No open-ended passivity here. Many researchers like this more aggressive approach to understanding.

The experiment has many advantages over fieldwork. The researcher has much more control. The booming and buzzing of reality are reduced to the absolute minimum possible. It is, in fact, the hallmark of an experiment that only one thing is able to change, and that change is under the researcher's control.

Consider, for example, the field research reported in my paper *Close Encounters* (Appendix B). As a field researcher, I had no control over what occurred in the restaurant. Because of this, I had very good validity but very low reliability. That means that what I described actually happened, but I had no idea if what I was seeing was at all typical, or if someone else would see a slightly different pattern than I did. If I had wanted to pursue the line of research indicated in this study, I could have moved into an experimental methodology. This is, in fact, the kind of progression that people called *grounded theorists* suggest: With a vague idea in mind, one goes out and looks at the world and then uses that look to refine the ideas, which, in turn, are used to allow a more precise view of reality. The experiment, in this instance, could provide a more precise view. It will certainly provide a *different* view.

Remember what the field study revealed about the differences in forms of public interaction between men and women. As in all fieldwork, the "environment" was messy. The ebb and flow of customers was dependent not on my needs but on the individual agendas of the customers and on the schedules of a number of different train, subway, and bus companies. There was no control over the number of people in the environment or over the male/ female ratio. Although the structure of the environment (the purpose it served, the arrangement of seating alternatives) was near perfect for my purposes, it was subject to far too many variables to make any precise testing of ideas possible.

Let's imagine that, in a small room on campus, I create a copy of the seating arrangement that was used in the Close Encounters Field Study. To distinguish this from the field study, I will refer to it as the Encounters Experiment. To duplicate some of the ambiance of the original environment, there could be coffee and tea available in urns and a box of pastries or donuts on an extra table. I could tell the students who were participating in the experiment that this room was just a waiting room and that the experiment itself would take place elsewhere. As far as the students would know, the room would be where they sat *prior* to getting involved in the experiment, but actually the room would be the real site of the experiment. This sort of trickery is almost inevitable in human experimentation.

The room could be equipped with audio recording devices so that all conversational exchanges would be recorded and with videotape recorders so that the seating sequences could be verified.

With this setup, I could control both the number of students and the male-female ratio in the research environment. I could control the sequence of entry into the room. To maximize control, it would be best to have everyone in the "waiting room" be part of the research team except for the one subject we would be testing. The members of the research team would pretend to be subjects and would seat themselves and interact according to a script. The use of colleagues would ensure that the environment that each of the real subjects entered would be exactly the same.

The only thing that would be out of my control would be what the students (called *subjects*) actually did once they walked into my little web. And that, of course, would be something that I would not want to control because it would be what I wanted to learn.

The attraction of the experiment should be obvious. First, what would be studied would be actual behavior. Granted, the behavior would not have taken place had the subjects not been put into a *simulated environment,* but the subjects would believe that the environment was real, so their behavior would be real as well. It would be *context defined,* but it would be real.

VARIABLES AND CONCEPTUALIZATIONS

In fieldwork, we use the hermeneutic circle to develop our ideas, understandings, and explanations. In experimentation, we use a

SIDEBAR 7.1 Experiments and Fieldwork

Contrast this Encounters Experiment with the sidewalk field experiment discussed in the previous chapter. The Encounters Experiment is a *laboratory* experiment. It is not that the experiment takes place in an actual lab but that we call the controlled environment used in an experiment a "laboratory." In contrast, the sidewalk experiment took place in an uncontrolled environment. It was not a *simulated* sidewalk, it was a real sidewalk. The "waiting room," on the other hand, is not a waiting room at all; it is a simulated waiting room. Therefore, the sidewalk study was a *field* rather than a *laboratory* experiment.

Also, the people in the sidewalk study were not subjects in any real sense, for they had not been recruited into the environment. These people, presumably, would have been on that sidewalk whether the experiment was conducted or not. That, of course, is not the case with the Encounters Experiment.

Finally, although all behavior is context defined, the behavior in a lab experiment is context defined at multiple levels. In the sidewalk experiment, the people acted within the context defined by their own lives and by their habitual sidewalk behavior. These things are the context that determines the way the people responded to the intruding pedestrian. In the fictional Encounters Experiment, the subjects also act within the context defined by their own lives and by their habitual behavior, but in addition there is an experimental context that colors the entire situation. The subjects in the Encounters Experiment know (or believe) that everyone else in the "waiting room" is also a volunteer in an experiment. This not only gives them something in common but may make them extremely conscious of their behavior—much like people in a waiting room prior to a job interview. The artificiality of this context threatens the validity of experimentation.

more traditional scientific approach, known as the *deductive model*. In traditional science, empirical research is not used to generate ideas. Instead, ideas are used to generate research by *deducing* what behavior would look like if a theory were accurate and then looking at the world to see if the predicted behavior actually occurs. This means that in an experiment, ideas are (as Bacon said) put to the test. To be tested, the ideas and the logic of the explanation must be clearly stated.

The ways the ideas are clarified are:

1. The topic being researched is reduced to variables.
2. Variables are operationalized.
3. The relationship between the variables is stated in terms of *hypotheses*.

The Variables

Remember: A variable is a collection of attributes. A variable is a classification scheme that is designed before it is tested. (In traditional science, thinking comes before looking.) This does not mean that the thinking cannot be based on previous experience, just that it cannot be based on the research it is designed to analyze. That is known as post hoc ("after the fact") analysis and is considered cheating because you are pretending to think before you look, but in fact you are peeking while thinking. This introduces a circularity (thinking, then peeking, then thinking, then looking) that is better suited to field methods.

An experiment is a *test* of an idea, so the idea must be clearly stated *prior* to the collection of data. The field study reported in *Close Encounters* began with a vague notion that the differences in the ethical norms of men and women would translate into different norms of public etiquette. But that is far too vague for an experiment.

If we used the room and design described above to turn the Close Encounters Field Study into the Encounters Experiment, we would basically have a *two-variable study.* This is known as a *two-by-two* design. We would be looking to see in what ways men and women differed in their forced interactions with strangers. We have two things that vary: (a) the sex of the subject and (b) the different ways of interacting. The variable "Sex" is easily divided into men and women, but the "Interaction" variable is somewhat trickier. With this variable, you have to make sure that the attributes are *mutually exclusive* and *exhaustive.* A good way of categorizing interaction into attributes would be to say that all the interactions were either *inclusive* or exclusive. The behavior identified with the women in the field study would be considered *inclusive* because the women tried to make contact with the people at their tables. The behavior associated with the men in the field study would be considered *exclusive* because the men attempted to create distance or barriers between themselves and their table mates.

OPERATIONALIZATION

These attributes need to be *operationalized* so that we know, when watching our subjects, whether we should say they are acting inclusively or exclusively. Recall from the Close Encounters Field Study the different ways people defined the connection between themselves and others: People turned either away from or toward the people around them. People created space for people by moving possessions out of the way. People touched or spoke with the people at the table. People acknowledged others with eye contact, a nod, or a smile.

Given that there are all these different ways of making or avoiding contact when sharing a table, there are two things a researcher can do. The first is to simplify the "Interaction" variable by operationalizing "inclusion" as "talking" and "exclusion" as "not talking." With these operationalizations, anyone who talks to another person is seen as inclusive, and anyone who doesn't is seen as exclusive. This would work, but we would miss a lot of the

Table 7.1 Interaction Scale

Variables	Attributes or Values	
Initiating Talk	Yes	No
Acknowledging Others	Yes	No
Touching	Yes	No
Facing Others	Faces toward	Faces away

nuances of social interaction. (Remember: By reducing life to variables, you are always losing some information.)

The second option would be to turn the "Interaction" variable into a scale. A *scale* is a variable that has attributes that can be interpreted as being more or less of some quality. (Scales will be discussed in more detail in Chapter 8.) An Interaction Scale could consist of variables that would measure all the possible types of interactions mentioned above. It would look like the one shown in Table 7.1.

Each of the attribute's positive answers ("yes" or "faces") would be worth 1 point; negative answers would be counted as 0. Using this formula, you can see that the range of possible points runs from 0 to 4. A subject would get 0 points if he or she didn't initiate talk, acknowledge others, or touch others and if he or she faced away. A subject would get 4 points if he or she did initiate talk, acknowledge others, touch others, and face others. This means that the attributes or values of the "Interaction" variable are the numerals 0 through 4: The higher the value, the greater the interaction.

Each of the scale variables is a *binomial* variable. A binomial variable is one that has only two choices: yes or no, male or female, pass or fail, win or lose, face toward or face away.

Let's look at a few *coding sheets* used to evaluate subjects taking part in the experiment (see Figure 7.1). Subject 1 has an Interaction score of 1. Subject 2 has an Interaction score of 3. Subject 3 has an Interaction score of 2.

RECORD NUMBER:	(MALE)	FEMALE
Variables	*Attributes or Values*	
Initiating Talk	Yes	(No)
Acknowledging Others	(Yes)	No
Touching	Yes	(No)
Facing Others	Faces Toward	(Faces Away)

RECORD NUMBER:	(MALE)	FEMALE
Variables	*Attributes or Values*	
Initiating Talk	(Yes)	No
Acknowledging Others	(Yes)	No
Touching	Yes	(No)
Facing Others	(Faces Toward)	Faces Away

RECORD NUMBER:	MALE	(FEMALE)
Variables	*Attributes or Values*	
Initiating Talk	Yes	(No)
Acknowledging Others	(Yes)	No
Touching	Yes	(No)
Facing Others	(Faces Toward)	Faces Away

Figure 7.1. Examples of Coding Sheets

You can see how the Encounters Experiment is much more reductionist than the field study. You can also see how it is possible to state precise differences by reducing complex behavior to numerical scores. With a good sample and a reasonable number of subjects, we could say something like "The mean (average) interaction score is 3.25 for women and 1.94 for men. Using the chi-square test, this difference is significant at the .001 level." See how much more scientific that sounds than the report from the fieldwork study? The experiment gives us a precise quantifiable difference, and this allows us to indicate how much credence we should give the data. Tests of statistical significance like the chi-square test tell us the likelihood that the results could be due to pure chance. In this fictional case, the number .001 means that these results could occur by chance in only one in every thousand cases, which means we can trust our findings.

You can end up with the same conclusions—for example, that women are more inclusive than men—using both field and experimental methods, but the experimental conclusion sounds much more scientific and reliable. So in this sense, you can think of different research methodologies as being *rhetorical strategies,* some being more convincing to different audiences than others. You can see that the Encounters Experiment would be a very expensive, labor-intensive undertaking. The payoff would be the statistical generalizability of the study. The cost would be the loss of validity.

RELATIONSHIPS AND HYPOTHESES

When we divide our area of interest into variables, we are not simply saying, in this example, that so many of our subjects are women or that so many of our subjects use an inclusive communication style. We are trying to say that there is something about being a man or a woman that has something to do with whether one is inclusive or exclusive. Speaking loosely, we could say that we believe there is a *causal connection* between the two variables. I say, "speaking loosely" because it is very difficult to make sense of causal statements about human beings. We don't want to say that being a woman *makes* you like this or that being a man *causes* you to be like that. That sort of causality is difficult to apply to creatures who occasionally think and who act purposefully.

SIDEBAR 7.2 Cause and Effect

In the social sciences, we tend to shy away from saying that anything *causes* anything else. Rather, we say that something *explains* something else or is *associated* or *correlated* with something else. This is not because we are trying to be vague but because the sorts of variables we are talking about are difficult to think of as causal and because the idea of causality is seriously flawed, especially when applied to human behavior.

When the word *cause* is used, it refers to the effect one variable has on another. Thus, "Increases in educational attainment cause increases in income." We all know there is no strict causality in this relationship. A beginning fast food worker with 2 years of college starts off at the same wage as a beginning fast food worker with 2 years of high school, and neither gets a raise at the completion of each semester.

The relationships discussed in the social sciences are always the relationships between abstract variables. The causality we mention is equally abstract.

Dependent and Independent Variables

When we talk about a relationship between variables, we usually discuss it in terms of *independent* and *dependent* variables. An independent variable is the one that influences the dependent variable. The *independent* variable is also known as the *causal* or *input* variable. The *dependent* variable is also known as the *outcome* variable. In the example we have been using, the independent variable is the sex of the subject, and the dependent variable is the subject's interaction style (inclusive or exclusive). In doing this research, we would argue that "Interaction Style" *is dependent on* "Sex." Or, put another way, if we know the sex of the sub-

SIDEBAR 7.3 Dependent and Independent Variables

One easy way to remember the difference between a dependent and independent variable is to think about *clouds* and *rain.* Rain is dependent on clouds (if there's rain, there must be clouds). But clouds are independent of rain (there can be clouds when it is not raining).

ject, we can predict (guess more accurately or be willing to bet on) the subject's interaction style.

The *prediction* has to be based in some sort of idea or *theory* about the way the world is. Let's imagine that we run the Encounters Experiment and find a very strong association between sex and interaction style. The mean (average) interaction score for men is 1.94, and the mean (average) score for women is 3.25. (Remember: These are imaginary data based on the scale discussed above that had a range from 0 to 4.) This would mean that women are more inclusive than men. If *predict* means "guess more accurately," then it is possible to predict a person's interaction style if you know his or her sex—but the opposite would also be true! If you know that someone is high on the interaction scale, then you can predict (that is, guess more accurately) that the person is a woman. The problem is that if you use "Interaction" to predict "Sex," then "Interaction" is the independent variable and "Sex" is the dependent variable. And this could lead to some confusion.

Saying that a variable is independent is saying that there is something about the variable that causes or creates the value in the outcome variable. There is something about being a woman (biology, educational attainment, socioeconomic status, power differences, or cultural status) that renders one more inclusive than men. It would be very odd, on the other hand, to say that there is something about being an inclusive person that renders one a woman.

Hypotheses: The Relationship
Between Data and Ideas

You can see from this example that it is our ideas that make one variable independent and another dependent. Look at a more plausible example. People have argued that low self-esteem results in low educational achievement. The argument is that people who have low self-esteem will not believe that it is possible to succeed, so they will not try. Their lack of effort will result in low levels of achievement and thus confirm their low self-esteem. In this model, self-esteem is the independent variable, and educational achievement is the dependent variable. There are other people who think the arguments about self-esteem are a lot of hooey. These people would argue that self-esteem does not cause achievement; rather, self-esteem is the result of achievement. Thus, those who do well think well of themselves, and those who do poorly think poorly of themselves. In this model, achievement is the independent variable, and self-esteem is the dependent variable. Look at Table 7.2 to see how this works.

It does not make sense to ask which view is the real one or which model is true. Models are just more or less useful. A philosopher named R. G. Collingwood (1962) once said that what we are calling independent variables are the variables we think we can most easily manipulate. Regardless of the model you think makes the most "sense," there will be people with low self-esteem who are high achievers and people with high self-esteem who are low achievers. In general, however, we will find that people who are high in one are high in the other. To say that it is one way or the other, you need both a solid argument about the relationship between the two variables *and* evidence that does not show that your argument is false. By itself, the evidence shows only that there is *some* connection; the direction of that connection is a matter of argument.

The hypothesis states what you expect to find once you look at the world. If you do not have a clear hypothesis, then you cannot have a valid experiment. To see how hypotheses are used to orga-

Table 7.2 Variables and Theoretical Perspectives

	Liberal Model	Conservative Model
Idea	Self-esteem is a subjective, psychological quality that affects performance.	Self-esteem is a subjective aspect of a social condition that is based on perceptions of performance.
Variables	Self-esteem is independent. Performance is dependent.	Self-esteem is dependent. Performance is independent.
Manipulation	To raise achievement, raise self-esteem.	To raise self-esteem, raise achievement.

nize research, we will look at an experiment by Michael Beatty and Ralph Behnke (1991) that tries to sort out whether public speaking anxiety is a personality trait or a situational reaction.

The argument concerning public speaking anxiety is based in two commonplace observations. First, all people feel public speaking anxiety in *some* speaking situations. Second, some people feel public speaking anxiety in *almost all* speaking situations. Those who feel anxious in *all* speaking situations are called apprehensive speakers, and those who are generally relaxed in most speaking situations are called nonapprehensive speakers.

Some of the research on public speaking anxiety is based on a comparison between scores on a public speaking anxiety trait questionnaire and the subject's heart rate during an actual speaking activity. The trait questionnaire supposedly measures whether a person is the "kind of person" (this is what *trait* means) who experiences high levels of anxiety when speaking in public. The score on this trait questionnaire is the independent variable in these studies, and it forms two attributes: apprehensive and nonapprehensive speakers.

The dependent variable or outcome measure is the amount of anxiety a person actually experiences. In the research tradition drawn on by Beatty and Behnke, anxiety has been operationalized as one's heart rate during a speech activity. This is similar to the way "lying" is operationalized on a lie-detector machine.

Beatty and Behnke saw that the researchers using these measures had mixed results. Some studies showed that those who were identified as apprehensive speakers tended to have higher heart rates during speaking activities than those identified as nonapprehensive. Other studies showed that there was no difference in heart rates between apprehensive and nonapprehensive individuals. Beatty and Behnke believed this was because some of the studies used situations in which almost everyone would experience some anxiety (e.g., videotaped formal presentations in front of large groups of hostile strangers), whereas other researchers used situations in which only people identified as apprehensive speakers would experience anxiety (e.g., informal discussion in small groups made up of familiar people). They called the conditions that would make most people anxious "high-intensity conditions" and the less apprehension-producing conditions "low-intensity conditions." On the basis of the literature they had read, Beatty and Behnke proposed the following hypotheses, which are stated exactly as they appeared in the article:

H1: Under low-intensity conditions, the heart rates of apprehensive speakers will be significantly higher than those of nonapprehensive speakers.

H2: Under high-intensity conditions, the heart rates of apprehensive speakers will not be significantly higher than those of nonapprehensive speakers.

H3: The heart rates of nonapprehensive speakers will be higher under high-intensity conditions than those of nonapprehensive speakers performing under low-intensity conditions.

H4: The heart rates of apprehensive speakers performing under high-intensity conditions will be significantly higher than those of apprehensive speakers performing under low-intensity conditions. (pp. 155-156)

Why all these hypotheses? Let's look at each one of them.

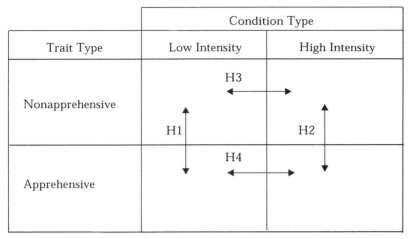

Figure 7.2. Visualizing Hypotheses

The first one, H1, is really the crucial one. It tells us that apprehensive speakers will be apprehensive in situations in which most people feel little or no anxiety. H2 tells us that we can expect both apprehensive and nonapprehensive speakers to experience anxiety in high-intensity situations. After all, that is why they are called "high-intensity situations." H3 is added because the comparison in H2 would make little sense unless nonapprehensive speakers were relaxed in low-intensity situations and anxious in high-intensity situations. H4 suggests that even though apprehensive speakers are anxious in all speaking situations, they are more anxious in high-intensity than in low-intensity situations.

Figure 7.2 shows how these comparisons look on a diagram of a two-by-two study. Read each of the hypotheses, and see how the lines indicate the comparisons being made.

You can see that all meaningful comparisons are being made. The predicted results are shown in Table 7.3.

I said that all meaningful comparisons were being made in the hypotheses. You can see that in Figure 7.2 there are no diagonal comparisons. That is because any comparison between nonapprehensives in low-intensity situations with apprehensives in

Table 7.3 Using a Two-by-Two Table to Clarify Ideas

	Situation Type	
Trait Type	Low Intensity	High Intensity
Nonapprehensive	Low anxiety	High anxiety
Apprehensive	Moderately high anxiety	High anxiety

high-intensity situations (or any other diagonal comparison) is attempting to make two comparisons simultaneously. The mark of an experiment, you'll recall, is that we manipulate one variable at a time. Thus, in H1 the authors are looking only at low-intensity conditions and letting trait type vary. This is known as holding conditions *constant*. Conditions are also held constant in H2, where the authors look only at high-intensity conditions and, again, let trait type vary. In H3 and H4, trait type is held constant, and condition is allowed to vary. These are the allowable types of comparisons.

Look at some hypotheses from different studies:

- As similarity between the speaker's speech rate and the listener's speech rate increases, perception of the speaker's social attractiveness will increase (Buller, LePoire, Aune, & Elroy, 1992, p. 290).
- As speaker's speech rate increases, perceptions of dominance and competence will increase (Buller et al., 1992, p. 290).
- Women will be less accepting of rape myths and more likely to regard acquaintance rape as an important social problem

than will men (Wilson, Linz, Donnerstein, & Stipp, 1992, p. 187).

- Standard-accented and fast-talking speakers will be upgraded on scales of competence but downgraded on scales of benevolence in relation to their nonstandard-accented and slow-talking counterparts (Giles, Henwood, Coupland, Harriman, & Coupland, 1992, p. 504).
- Adolescent viewers of "Channel One" (a commercial, educational program used in secondary schools) will express more materialistic attitudes than nonviewers (Greenberg & Brand, 1993, p. 144).

You can see that these are all stated as if they were facts. You also know, because experimenters are scientists and scientists think before they look, that these hypotheses are developed before the researcher knows whether they are accurate. It is because of this quality of hypotheses—that they state as fact what we do not yet know—that science is seen as predictive.

EXPERIMENTAL MODELS

Experiments come in three basic designs: descriptive (or *univariate*), explanatory/stimulus, and explanatory/subjects. We will look at each of these (Table 7.4).

Descriptive Experiments

Perhaps the most famous descriptive experiment was Stanley Milgram's (1974) torture experiment. In this experiment, subjects were told they were part of a study looking at memory and learning. Subjects were introduced in pairs, one of whom would be randomly selected to be the "teacher" and the other the "learner." In fact, the "learner" was a confederate of the researcher, and all the subjects played the role of teacher. The "teachers"

Table 7.4 Experimental Models

Type of Study	Environment	Subjects	Outcome Measure
Descriptive	No variation	No variation	Variation
Explanatory stimulus	Variation	No variation	Variation
Explanatory subjects	No variation	Variation	Variation

were told to ask the learners, located out of sight in another room, to recall information that had been given earlier and to shock the learner with electricity each time the learner answered incorrectly. At each wrong answer, the teacher provided a more painful shock, and after a while the unseen learner would scream in pain and beg the teacher to stop. Finally, the learner stopped responding at all, implying that the pain had rendered him unconscious or worse.

In reality, the learner was not being shocked at all. But the subjects (the "teachers") were responding to the simulated environment in which they found themselves acting as torturers.

This is a univariate study because no comparisons were being made. *Univariate,* as you would imagine, means "one variable." The research question being asked here is whether people will torture innocent people for no apparent reason. (The answer, by the way, is that under certain circumstances, a great many will.) There is no attempt to explain the behavior by manipulating either the environment or the characteristics of the group of people being studied. The only variable is the outcome measure, and that, as discussed earlier, is in the control of the subjects. In this study, the outcome measure is the subject's willingness to torture strangers, which has been operationalized as the number of "shocks" the "teacher" gives to the "learner."

If you analyzed this study using Table 7.3, you would put down that the environment didn't change: All the subjects experienced the same objective reality. And because no information was provided indicating that different kinds or types of people were being studied, you would put down that there was no variation within the subjects studied. There were no comparisons, that is, between male and female "teachers," or between old and young, educated and uneducated, or anything else. Explanatory experiments deal with the relationship between an independent and a dependent variable, and because there is no independent variable, this cannot be an explanatory experiment.

Explanatory/Stimulus Experiments

The results of the Milgram experiment are frequently discussed in the framework of authority. Young men volunteered to participate in an experiment on the campus of a prestigious university. The experiment took place in a clinical environment under the direction of a university professor. This was an alien and intimidating environment for most of the young men, and it was entirely a natural environment for the professor. This results in what Milgram called an "agentic shift," in which individuals transfer responsibility for their actions to other people or institutions (such as the professor, the university, "science," or "knowl-edge").

Neil Postman, in his book *Technopoly* (1993), asserts that "Milgram's study was not empirical in the strict sense, since it was not based on observations of people in natural life situations" (p. 152). He goes on to say, "I assume that no one is especially interested in how people behave in laboratories at Yale or any other place; what matters is how people behave in situations where their behavior makes a difference to their lives" (p. 152). Postman is questioning the validity of Milgram's experiment, arguing that this sort of contextless behavior tells us very little about moral behavior.[1] Whether or not you accept all of Postman's argument, he throws in an interesting environmental question: "For myself, I feel quite sure that if each of Milgram's subjects had been required to read Hannah Arendt's *Eichmann in*

Jerusalem before showing up at the laboratory, his numbers would have been quite different" (p. 152).

To test this idea would require manipulating the environment by introducing a stimulus or an "intervention." In this case, the stimulus or intervention would be requiring some of the subjects to read Hannah Arendt's (1963) book about Nazi atrocities. Only *some* of the subjects could read the book because if *all* the subjects read the book then the environment would be identical for all the subjects and we would be back to a descriptive study (and a very odd one at that). To say that the environment is variable, we have to have different conditions. In this study, one condition would be reading the book, and the other would be not reading the book. Using the outcome measure, we would compare the subjects who read Arendt and those who didn't. We—or, at least, Postman—would expect that those who did read a moral analysis of Nazi behavior would be more self-conscious about their behavior and less willing to give strangers electric shocks.

Explanatory/Subjects Experiments

In the two models above, the assumption is that all human beings are basically alike. This is an unwarranted assumption, yet it permeates much of experimental research in the social and medical sciences. At the very least, there may be people who have already read *Eichmann in Jerusalem* or some similar book prior to becoming involved in the experiment. It may be that the people who read such books are already more predisposed to approach the world using a moral or ethical framework than those who don't. Instead of treating moral considerations as a stimulus, we could conceptualize moral frameworks as a form of intellectual culture. We could run the experiment as originally described and then compare people who read to people who do not.

The number of interesting comparisons is almost endless. We could use college students and compare humanities majors to science majors or to engineering students. Arguments have been made that American women have a more social morality than

American men, so this is a comparison that could be made. There are all sorts of cross-cultural comparisons that would be interesting, and a researcher could look at whether people who identified themselves as religious were any more or less likely to torture people than those who saw themselves in more secular terms. Social class might be a relevant variable: Are people in the upper middle class more or less likely than people in the lower classes to engage in the "agentic shifts" that Milgram mentions?

These and similar comparisons require that the objective experience of the subjects be unchanging. If the environment varies as the subjects vary, then it will not be clear if the differences in the environment are due to environmental stimuli or subject characteristics. And if you cannot say what is creating the differences in the outcome measure, then you do not have a coherent experimental design. The whole point of an experiment is to be clear. As Postman indicated, you are giving up an enormous amount of validity in exchange for clarity—so if you don't have clarity, you have nothing.

CONTROL GROUPS

Sometimes the connection between a stimulus and an outcome is not clear. This is especially the case when there is a lot of time involved in the experiment.

One of the basic experimental models is called *pretest-posttest* because it involves measuring the outcome variable at one point (the *pre*-test), then doing something (the stimulus or intervention), and then measuring the outcome measure again (the *post*-test) to see if it has changed. Example: Take a math test, take a math lesson, retake the math test.

One of the problems with this is that everyone retaking the math test has already taken it once. That alone may be enough to account for the improved scores on the second exam. What you may want to do is have a second group—a control group—that takes the first and second tests but does not get a math lesson.

Table 7.5 The Pretest-Posttest Model

	Pretest	*Intervention*	*Posttest*
Experimental group	Acts as teacher-torturer	Participates in philosophy seminar	Acts as teacher-torturer
Control group	Acts as teacher-torturer	No intervention	Acts as teacher-torturer

This group could go watch a rerun of *Flipper* while the experimental group takes its math lesson. If the control group's scores match the experimental group's scores, the lesson had no effect.

Let's imagine that we actually decide to test Postman's idea that reading moral philosophy makes people less inclined to torture others. We decide to use a pretest-posttest model. This means that we first run Milgram's torture experiment (the *pretest*), then run a 2-week seminar on moral philosophy, and then run a second torture experiment (the *posttest*) to see if the subjects have changed the way they behave.

The problem, as you can imagine, is that it would be difficult to get anyone to participate twice in Milgrim's experiment. And even if we could somehow force the subjects to participate twice, it is quite likely that the willingness to torture would *decline even without reading moral philosophy.* After all, Milgrim's experiment is based to a great degree on catching the subjects by surprise.

If we ran the moral philosophy version of the experiment without a control group, we might find that a large percentage of subjects would flatly refuse to participate in the experiment and that others would stop much earlier than before. Without a control group, it would be tempting, but obviously simplistic, to say that reading philosophy made all the difference—or even *any* of the difference. A control group would let us know how much of the difference was simply a result of having participated in the experiment and having time to think. Table 7.5 shows what the experimental design would look like.

Table 7.6 The Role of Control Groups: Scenario 1

	Average Pretest Score	*Intervention*	*Average Posttest Score*
Experimental group	50 acts of torture	Participates in philosophy seminar	20 acts of torture
Control group	49 acts of torture	No intervention	20 acts of torture

Table 7.7 The Role of Control Groups: Scenario 2

	Average Pretest Score	*Intervention*	*Average Posttest Score*
Experimental group	50 acts of torture	Participates in philosophy seminar	20 acts of torture
Control group	49 acts of torture	No intervention	33 acts of torture

The use of control groups would allow us to see to what extent our ideas concerning philosophy and torture are valid. The experimental results *could* look like what is shown in Table 7.6 or 7.7.

In Scenario 1 (Table 7.6), you can see that for the experimental group, the number of torturous acts dropped from 50 to 20. This is a substantial drop, and we would all run out and advocate the importance of philosophy if we didn't have the control group to curb our enthusiasm. The control group in Scenario 1 started off with roughly the same number of torturous acts as the experimental group. The control group also reduced the number of torturous acts to the same level as the experimental group *without the benefit of the intervention.*

Scenario 2 (Table 7.7) shows a fictitious situation in which the experimental group lowers its willingness to torture to a greater extent than does the control group.

What does each scenario tell us? The first scenario tells us that for those who have already realized that they were capable of "torturing" someone, reading philosophy does little good. Because the control group torture rates also went down, it appears that anything that forces people to think about ethical issues is effective in producing ethical behavior and that participation in the experiment itself was enough to make people consider the ethical dimensions of their behavior. This *experimental effect* is also called the *Pygmalion effect* and comes into play when the experiment itself alters what it is attempting to measure.

The second scenario posits results that show that although there is some experimental effect, there is a greater intervention effect, indicating that reading philosophy does help alter people's behavior.

Although the pretest-posttest design is extremely common, especially in psychological and social-psychological approaches to research, another method may be simpler. The problem with the philosophy/torture experiment we have been describing is that it is difficult to separate out the experimental from the intervention effect. So let's think about *why* we want to do a pretest-posttest and *why* we need a control group.

- We need a pretest because we want to know whether the intervention has changed the subjects, and we cannot know whether the subjects have changed if we do not know what the subjects were like before the intervention took place.
- We need a control group to account for change due to the passage of time and the experimental effect.

One of the ways to deal with both of these issues is to use a *posttest-only control group design* (see Table 7.8).

The assumption in this model, which will be discussed in more detail in the section on sampling, is that for all practical purposes the people in the experimental group are indistinguishable from the people in the control group. This assumption is required for *all* control group designs because if the control group consists of

SIDEBAR 7.4 The Solomon Four-Group Design

The two designs discussed here—pretest-posttest and posttest only—do not exhaust the possibilities. The most rigid experimental design is the Solomon four-group. In the designs already discussed, subjects were divided into two groups (experimental and control) that were defined by two different experiences—either receiving the experimental intervention or not—and both the groups were involved in the pre- and posttests.

As the name suggests, there are four groups rather than two in the four-group design. As the table below indicates, in this design there are two experimental and two control groups.

Groups	Pretest	Intervention	Posttest
1	Yes	Yes	Yes
2	Yes	No	Yes
3	No	Yes	Yes
4	No	No	Yes

You will notice that Groups 1 and 2 cover the designs discussed in the text. Remember, the rationale for these two groups was that you wanted to make sure that it was the intervention, rather than either the experience of taking the pretest or the passage of time, that accounted for the differences (if any) in posttest results.

The Solomon four-group design adds Groups 3 and 4 as a sort of control overkill. Group 3, like Group 2, is designed to rule out any effects of the pretest. If the intervention creates the posttest differences, then the scores of Groups 1 and 3 should be similar (i.e., not statistically different). And if the intervention creates the posttest differences, then the posttest scores of Groups 2 and 4 should be similar.

If your hypothesis is correct in your experiment, then Groups 1 and 3 should be substantially the same *and* substantially different from Groups 2 and 4.

This is an extremely rigid design and results in data that allow for a clearer, and more definitive, interpretation.

Table 7.8 The Posttest-Only Model

	Pretest	Intervention	Posttest
Experimental group	None	Participates in philosophy seminar	Acts as teacher-torturer
Control group	None	No intervention	Acts as teacher-torturer

people who are fundamentally different from those in the experimental group, then the design makes no sense.

If the people in the control and experimental groups are, for the purposes of research, essentially the same, then the control group results can serve the same purpose as the pretest results in the pretest-posttest design. The pretest was designed to tell us what *these* (kinds of) people were like prior to the intervention. Because the control group members are the same kind of people and because, by definition, the control group does not get the intervention, we don't need to do a pretest.

By cutting out the pretest, not only do you drastically reduce the experimental effect, but you also cut costs considerably, and you eliminate the problem of *attrition* (people who take the pretest but drop out before taking the posttest).

SAMPLING IN EXPERIMENTS

The rules for sampling in experiments are governed by the limitations of experimental designs. The key limitation of experiments is the small sample size. Small sample size, as you'll remember from the Chapter 4, tends to exaggerate individual differences. This exaggeration results in data in which a very small number of people can distort the findings so that the group's performance on the outcome measure is unlikely to be representative of the population.

Remember, sample size is related to *cell* size. If you want to run an experiment with 100 subjects and you have a control group, then your sample size is 50 per cell. If you also want to compare men and women, then your cell size is down to 25. Keep this in mind. The number of people in all the cells put together may not be the most important number.

Another difficulty in sampling in experiments is that participation in experiments is time consuming. The people studied in ethnographic fieldwork are not inconvenienced at all. The people studied in telephone or mail surveys are hardly inconvenienced— an interruption, a small amount of time. But to participate in an experiment means, for the most part, that you have to be selected and pretested and willing to go to the experimental site. This means that it is more difficult to get a representative sample. This is also why experiments are so often conducted on captive audiences: prisoners, patients, students, poor people, and soldiers.

The small numbers usually involved in experiments and the problem with recruiting subjects mean that random sampling is generally not possible. The exception to this, of course, is if one has a really captive audience and the researcher has the power to force people to participate. Forcing people to participate in experiments, however, is both unethical and illegal.

Because random sampling is largely not used in experimental research, the best sampling design is *purposive sampling.* This is, as you can imagine, sampling for a specific purpose. It means that instead of using a random selection process, a researcher draws the sample from the group of people he or she wishes to study. This involves an assumption, common in experimental research, that aside from the quality in which the researcher is interested, all people are pretty much interchangeable. So if a researcher wants conduct an experiment with midlevel managers in large corporations, it becomes irrelevant whether those managers are men or women, black or white, young or old, Jews or Hindus,

SIDEBAR 7.5 Researcher Bias and the Double-Blind Design

We tend to see what we want to see.

Experimental research is quantitative and variable analytic. Reality is neither quantitative nor composed of variables, so the difficulty we have is in imposing a form of analytic order on the world.

Operationalization, as you now know, sets up the rules by which we categorize the world: how we count it and which things we put into which boxes. But operationalization never can be so fine as to exclude judgment. Anyone with experience in empirical research is aware of the judgment calls that are being made in following the rules of operationalization. Research methods were formalized precisely because of this awareness.

One of the ways to control researcher bias is to design experiments as *double-blind*. This means that neither the researchers nor the subjects know who is in the experimental group and who is in the control group.

This is a methodology frequently used in drug testing. The subjects are not told whether they are receiving an actual drug or a useless but identical-looking *placebo*. This is done for two reasons: to control for a Pygmalion effect and to get volunteers. It would be difficult to get people to volunteer to

Republicans or Democrats—all that matters is that they are mid-level managers in large corporations.

Selection into experimental and control groups must be done randomly. Each subject could be given a number and the numbers drawn randomly by computer. A less technically advanced and equally good method would be to have numbered slips of paper in a hat. Each subject could draw a number, and all odd numbers could be in the control group. Random means random, and any means of random selection is valid.

not get any medical help—and such people would most likely be substantially dissimilar from those who actually wanted help.

The researchers are not told who is getting the real drugs and who is not in order to prevent overly optimistic interpretations of those receiving the drugs and to prevent treatment differences between the experimental and control groups.

There are obviously ethical considerations in double-blind experiments like these. Researchers must design experiments in which seriously ill people (people with AIDS, for example) are condemned to spend years taking sugar pills rather than experimental drugs. On the other hand, of course, the drugs are *experimental*, which means that those taking placebo drugs are not subjected to potentially dangerous, possibly useless medications.

Double-blind experiments are used less often in communication and social scientific research because the need for control is not as crucial. At the same time, the room for interpretation is frequently both huge and subtle in communication research. For this reason, research assistants and subjects are usually kept blind to the purpose of the research.

CONFIDENTIALITY AND ANONYMITY

Social science research is not about individuals. Social scientists study the way people behave *in general* or the way *certain groups* of people or *types* of people behave. A person's individual identity, apart from its role as representative of certain variables, is irrelevant to the research. This means that the research should not know any more about the subjects than is required by the study. Either the identity of the subjects should be confidential, or the subjects should be anonymous.

When we say that a subject's identity is *confidential,* we mean that we know who he or she is but we will not tell anyone. The subject's identity will be held in *confidence.* When we say that a subject's participation in a study is *anonymous,* we mean that we do not know who the person is.

In the double-blind studies discussed above, information about the subjects was withheld from both the researchers and the subjects to protect the integrity of the research. The issues of confidentiality and anonymity have less to do with the quality of the research than with the rights of the subjects. Confidentiality and anonymity are ethical considerations—and not ethical in an abstract, philosophical fashion. Research conducted at a university or with federal funds must conform to certain ethical guidelines. This includes student research. Research conducted outside of a university setting or with the use of government funds should conform to the professional standards that are associated with research disciplines. The American Psychological Association, the American Medical Association, the American Sociological Association, the American Anthropological Association, and other associations of people in research professions have published guidelines that should be followed.

The philosophical basis for these ethical guidelines can probably be traced back almost infinitely, but I think these sorts of considerations are most succinctly based in Immanuel Kant's idea that human beings are "ends in themselves" rather than a means to someone else's ends. Translated from philosophy into English, this means that you cannot *use* people for your own purposes, no matter what those purposes may be.

Confidentiality and Anonymity in the Experimental Setting

Regulating ethical considerations often results in contradictions. In an experiment, subjects are required to give what is called "informed consent." This means that the subjects must know, more or less, what is going to happen to them. The re-

Table 7.9 Data Sheet From Survey

REC-NUMB	PROD-UCT	COM-TYPE	IN-DUST	GROWTH	COM-SIZE	FIVE-AGO	PER-CENT	F-TEMP	P-TEMP
601	HEATING	1	5	2	4	4	40	95	5
602	CHILDABU	1	12	3	3	1		30	70
603	LEGALSER	1	12	2	1	1	25	100	
604	TX PROG	1	12	3	6	4		80	20
605	MOSQCONT	2	11	2	3	3	0	61	
606	OLIVEOIL	1	2	3	3	2	5	75	25
607	FINANCIA	2	4	2	4	4	0	90	10
608	MED BILL	1	11	3	5	4	25	100	
609	BANKSER	2	4	3	4	3	40	90	10

searcher must keep records of signed informed-consent forms, and this means that there is a record of each subject's participation in the experiment. These forms must be kept secure. *Secure* means that they should be locked away. Locking them away ensures confidentiality. Different institutions have different rules, but generally these forms should be destroyed after a certain number of years.

Although it may seem that anonymity is a higher standard than confidentiality, the two are not really mutually exclusive. Keeping the subjects' identities confidential does not preclude keeping the data anonymous. If there is no way to link the data to any particular person, then the data are anonymous. Table 7.9 shows data from a survey, but data from an experiment will look very much like this. You can see that there is nothing on this sheet that tells us who respondent number 601 is.

Research ethics is a complicated and nuanced area of concern, and we cannot go into tremendous depth in this text. You should, however, understand that life is not so simple that one can say that "either the data are anonymous or they are not." If you know that a friend of yours was involved in this experiment, and you get an opportunity to see the data or read the report, you will know that your friend was *one of the people* described in the study. If there were only, say, 50 people in the study and half were women, then you know that your friend was one of the 25 men described. Any other descriptive variables will further narrow this even more. Usually, this is not a big deal, but imagine that the experiment was about drug use, deviant sex, criminal activity, or some other socially sensitive issue. Think about this: You have to be very careful. People are an end in themselves.

WRITING

The key to writing about experimentation is clarity. Because experimentation is the most formal of the scientific methods discussed in this text, the writing will also be the most formal. If we contrast fieldwork with experimentation, we can see that fieldwork is much more *exploratory,* whereas experimentation is much more of a *test of ideas.* Because it is a test, we have to be very clear on what is being tested and on what will count as support for the test. You should also keep in mind that experimentation is the method most likely to be replicated (because replication is more a part of experimental values than it is for other methods). Because of the idea of research as a test and the idea of likely replication, when you write about an experimental study you have to make sure that people know *exactly* what you did. Think of writing about an experiment as writing a set of instructions for how to conduct a replication.

COMMENTS

Ethical Issues

In fieldwork, the subjects are going about their normal activities—or at least they are not doing things because the researcher wants them to—and because of this, privacy is the major ethical issue. In experimentation, on the other hand, the subjects are being manipulated by the researcher. This manipulation raises major ethical issues.

Confidentiality and anonymity have already been discussed in this chapter, as has the issue of informed consent. These do not need to be discussed in any more detail here except to say that colleges and universities will have specific guidelines concerning these and other ethical issues raised by all research methods.

What makes experimentation particularly sensitive to ethical questions is that it involves manipulating subjects and that it quite often requires some element of deception. It does not help matters that experimentation in the social sciences has a history that includes some shockingly abusive experiments. The basic rules of experimental ethics are that (a) subjects give their informed consent; (b) subjects' identities are kept confidential; (c) subjects are not physically, mentally, or emotionally mistreated; and (d) subjects are debriefed following their participation in the experiment.

What counts as physical, mental, or emotional mistreatment is open to interpretation. While working at a research institution, I saw the Human Subjects Committee decide that videotaping poor patients during physical examinations was not overly intrusive but that letting some physicians watch a video presentation rather than an in-person presentation was a mistreatment of the physician-subjects. Because treatment of experimental subjects is so dependent on values and perspectives, universities generally require that approval be obtained from some committee on the grounds that it is better to have the judgment of more than one person.

Debriefing refers to the process in which a subject is told in more detail about the experiment in which he or she just participated. Debriefing is designed both to be informative and to deal with emotional issues raised by the participation. The point of debriefing is to bring closure to the experiment. In a debriefing, the researcher explains to the subjects the point of the experiment and tries to answer whatever questions the subjects have.

SIDEBAR 7.6 Vocabulary		
Anonymity	Binomial variable	Cell
Coding sheet	Confidentiality	Constant
Control groups	Deductive model	Dependent variable
Descriptive experiment	Double-blind	Experimental effect
Explanatory experiment	Hypothesis	Independent variable
Inductive model	Input variable	Intervention
Outcome variable	Placebo	Post hoc
Posttest	Posttest-only	Prediction
Pretest	Purposive sampling	Pygmalion effect
Solomon four-group		

Connections

We have already seen that experiments can be used in field settings as well as in the more traditional laboratories. Experiments are also linked to survey research in that quite often the variables being manipulated are reactions to survey questions rather than actual changes in behavior. When this is the case, the researcher has to follow the guidelines for survey development discussed in the following chapter. The rationales for using survey measurements rather than behavioral measurements are that it solves some of the reliability issues (coding behavior is frequently quite tricky), is more practical (takes less time and costs less), and runs a lower risk of violating ethical norms. It also, however, takes on some of the limitations of surveys, which are discussed in the following chapter.

▓ ACTIVITIES AND EXERCISES

1. You think that people judge each other more or less harshly depending on the perceived seriousness of the action being judged and the perceived motivation of the wrongdoer. Design an experiment to test these ideas. *Think:* What are the variables? What variable(s) is/are independent? Dependent? *Remember:*

SIDEBAR 7.7 Excerpt From "Cross-Cultural Comparison of Implicit Theories of Requesting," by Min-Sun Kim and Steven R. Wilson (1994, p. 210)

The primary aim of this paper is to identify cross-cultural similarities and differences in people's implicit theories of requesting. Implicit theories are conceptualized as containing information about five interactive constraints that influence choices about requests: (1) Clarity, (2) Perceived imposition, (3) Consideration for the other's feelings, (4) Risking disapproval for self, and (5) Effectiveness. The paper compares how these five constraints are perceived and rated across cultures and traces possible links between the constraints and perceptions of the likelihood of using various request strategies. Participants are a total of 595 undergraduates: 296 Koreans (native speakers of Korean) and 299 Americans (native American English speakers) studying in their respective countries. After reading a hypothetical request situation, participants evaluated request strategies along the five constraint dimensions as well as for likelihood of use. The rank-ordering of the request strategies along the dimensions were similar across cultures except for effectiveness of strategies. Striking cross-cultural differences were found in the rank and mean strategy ratings for effectiveness judgments: U.S. participants considered the direct statement strategy as the most effective way of making a request, while Korean participants rated it as the least effective strategy. Regarding the incompatibility among interactive constraints, U.S. participants saw clarity to be closely related to effectiveness of strategies; for Korean participants clarity of strategies was counterproductive to effectiveness. Theoretical and practical implications of these findings are discussed.

Overview [of methods, following the theoretical discussion and review of the relevant literature]

The main purpose of this study was to test three hypotheses about cross-cultural similarities and differences in implicit theories of requesting. After a series of pilot tests, experi-

(Continued)

SIDEBAR 7.7 Continued

mental participants were randomly provided with a questionnaire containing one of the six situations with one of the two
sets of 12 exemplar tactics (which instantiated the three request strategies) for that situation and were asked to evaluate the tactics along the five dimensions of constraints as
well as for perceived likelihood of use.

In an experiment you create a situation in which real behavior is
observed—you do not ask people what they think.

2. You think that it is not gender that determines speech behavior
such as interruptions so much as power differences based on
social status. Design an experiment to test this idea.

3. What do you think?

In the article quoted above, the claim is made that this
is an experiment. In what sense is this an experiment, and
in what sense is it not one? With the understanding that
you do not have the complete article, what are Kim and
Wilson (1994) trying to find out? How would you rate their
approach in terms of reliability and validity?

What other methods could you use to get at the problem Kim and Wilson are investigating? How would they
compare to this approach in terms of both reliability and
validity?

Find another article that deals with a related issue, and
compare its approach to the approach of this article.

NOTE

1. Postman's remarks also need to be put into context. Postman was not arguing that Milgram's experiment was flawed. He was making the much stronger
argument that all social scientific experiments are invalid. He stated,
"[Milgram's] study—which, incidentally, I find both fascinating and terrify-
ing—is not science. It is something else entirely" (p. 153).

8

SURVEYS

We have looked at fieldwork and at experimental research. Fieldwork allows us to study how people actually behave in real-life situations, and experimental research allows us to study how people act and think in manipulated or relatively artificial situations. These two methods vary according to the amount of control the researcher has and differ in terms of reliability and validity.

The choice of methods, however, is not based on abstract considerations or personal preferences alone: Some questions can best be answered using a particular methodology. Questions about behavior, for example, are best answered with fieldwork or experimental designs. This is because, as we all know, what we say is only loosely related to what we actually do—if it's related at all. Think back to the Milgram experiment: How many people do you think would have admitted that they would be willing to torture people? How many of the people who actually did "torture" people in that experiment would have known in advance?

On the other hand, some of what we want to know does not involve behavior. When we are interested in values, opinions, perceptions, concerns, ideas, or attitudes, we can—with a great deal of caution—simply ask people what they are thinking. If we are

asking questions that can be answered in this way, then we are using a methodology known as *survey research.*

Survey research involves asking people questions and accepting their answers as data. The questions can be asked in face-to-
face interviews, in telephone surveys, or in questionnaires sent by
mail.

THE RELIABILITY OF SURVEY RESEARCH

Survey research ranks very high on reliability. This is largely because it is a quantitative methodology. Being quantitative does
not mean that all surveys or all survey questions are reliable. It
does mean that *finding out* whether they are reliable is a fairly
straightforward matter.

Reliability in surveys, like the reliability discussed in the chapters on fieldwork and experimentation, concerns the ability of the
research to be *replicated.* Surveys, like experiments, are easily repeated because it is possible to exactly duplicate both the data
collection (the questions asked) and the sampling design. Survey
researchers, like experimenters, have a great deal of control.

One of the things that must be kept in mind about surveys is
that they are a product of modern technology. Without computers and telephones, survey research would be virtually impossible. In fact, survey research shows how technology can radically
change our ideas about society and about what is considered
knowledge. There are some drawbacks to this, as we will see in
the discussion of validity, but one of the benefits is in the testing of
reliability.

Because reliability is the ability of a study to be replicated with
a different, but similar, sample of respondents, it is possible to use
the computer to split the sample into two or more groups and
treat them as replications. Instead of a sample of 900, for example, you could have your computer *randomly divide* the respondents into three subsamples of 300 each. Then you could com-

pare the pattern of answers from new subsamples. Because the samples were drawn using the same sampling design and because the new subsamples were sorted randomly, the pattern of answers should be substantially the same. If they are not, then the study lacks reliability.

This sort of internal check on reliability has a number of advantages over external reliability checks. Most obviously, it does not require the time and expense of drawing a new sample and conducting a new survey. Second, it avoids some of the problems of validity that occur when trying to recreate anything in a society that is continuously changing.

The Time Element

Surveys tend to be *cross-sectional* rather than *longitudinal*. That means that surveys are not generally designed to examine changes. Instead, surveys attempt to find out how people are thinking *at a given time.* This does not mean that a survey takes place in an instant of time, or even that it takes place in a very short amount of time. It means that the researcher ignores the element of time.

Sometimes this is not possible. I once conducted a survey to determine knowledge and attitudes about AIDS. I sent the surveys out in two waves, and just as the second wave went out, Magic Johnson, star basketball player and celebrity role model, announced that he was HIV positive. Though normally I could have treated the 6 week survey period as "one time period," Johnson's announcement destroyed any illusion that time was not a relevant factor in determining why people gave the answers that they did.

This AIDS survey was salvaged as a *longitudinal* study that documented (as it turned out) the lack of impact of Johnson's announcement on knowledge and attitudes about AIDS. A longitudinal study is one that takes time seriously as a variable and looks for changes in the responses the survey generates.

SIDEBAR 8.1 Time as a Variable

A *longitudinal* study is one in which time is a variable. The time at which any individual completes his or her survey is seen as relevant. In a cross-sectional study, all individuals are considered to have completed the questionnaire at the same time, even if the researcher knows that *a considerable amount of time passed between the completion of the first questionnaire and the completion of the last.* The time of completion is not seen as relevant. It is possible to combine surveys that were conducted over a number of years and treat them as if they were completed at the same time. This is sometimes done, for example, when one wants to look at specific population groups that make up only a small percentage of the population. I have a friend who combined a number of U.S. Census reports in order to track patterns among single female immigrants, a group too small to analyze using a single census.

The longer you wait between replications, the more it is likely that time will become relevant. Because of this, external replications are not as good as internal, subsample replications.

Types of Longitudinal Designs

There are three basic types of longitudinal studies: cohort, panel, and repeated cross-sectional. All of them are designed to look at change over time, but they sample in different ways.

A *cohort* study follows a group of people who have some sort of shared identity. We could begin a study of the college graduates of 1998 and follow this graduate "cohort" through their lives. Let's imagine that there are 50,000 college graduates in 1998 (this is an entirely fictitious number). To do this study as a cohort study, we would need a list of these graduates, and then we would periodically survey *some sample of this population.* We would not necessarily talk to the same individuals each time we surveyed the population. Instead, we would take a random sample that would represent the population. The theory is that any good sample of this cohort would represent the cohort. If attitudes changed over time, we could say that the attitudes of the members of this cohort had changed, even though probably there would be members we had never contacted and members we had contacted more than once.

A *panel study,* in contrast, looks at the *same individuals* each time a survey is conducted. We sometimes see this on the news during an election. A group of citizens is formed and then repeatedly interviewed to see how (or if) people's opinions are influenced by political and media events. This type of study is strong in that it allows you to ask specific individuals why they have changed (or not changed), but it has a few weaknesses as well. First, there is the problem of *attrition.* Attrition occurs when people are lost to the group. (The Vietnam War, for example, is called a "war of attrition" because winning and losing were defined in terms of the individuals lost to each side rather than the gaining or losing of territory.) Because the validity of a panel study hinges on the ability to recontact the same individuals, attrition is a major source of problems. The second problem is also a sampling problem, although it is less crucial than the problem of attrition. A panel study, because it repeatedly contacts the same members of a cohort, studies fewer members than does a cohort study.

Staying with the example of election coverage, *repeated cross-sectional studies* are often used to chart how the opinion of American voters changes in the course of an election campaign. These studies simply look at all voters (or "likely voters") as being the same, so any representative sample of voters will do. The "horse-race polls" that we see each election, telling us that so-and-so is ahead or behind, are based on repeated cross-sectional surveys.

VALIDITY

The question of validity is more complex.

In the introductory section of this chapter, it was said that surveys can be used to find out what people are thinking and how those thoughts relate to more concrete elements of their lives. In this way, surveys differ sharply from fieldwork and experimental designs. But the relationship between what people think they will do and what they actually will do is not necessarily a strong one. There is also a gap between what people *think* they are like and what they *actually* are like. Because of these discontinuities, it is a leap of faith to assume a strong connection between what people think and feel and what they *say* they think and feel.

This is especially true when a researcher looks at normative issues. Socially, it is easier to *say* you are bigoted than to actually *act* in a bigoted manner, but it is also easier to *think* bigoted thoughts than to *write them down* on a questionnaire or to tell them to an interviewer. This is the problem of *socially preferred answers:* People will shade their responses toward what they think are the researcher's biases or toward what they believe will put them in a better light. People do not like to look bad or ignorant—or to think of themselves as bad or ignorant. This means that what people say may not be a valid indication of people's attitudes.

ASKING QUESTIONS

> *A young monk was once rebuffed by his superior when he asked if he could smoke while he prayed. Ask a different question, a friend advised. Ask if you can pray while you smoke.*
>
> Crossen (1994, p. 28)

Another major source of invalidity on questionnaires comes from the questions themselves. Cynthia Crossen, in her book *Tainted Truth* (1994), talks about two ways researchers have looked at television-viewing habits:

SIDEBAR 8.2 What Is Being Measured?

There is also the highly relevant philosophical question of what it means to say that people think or feel anything at all during the times in which they are not actively, consciously thinking and feeling. For example, the only time you may ever think about the vice president of the United States or about the appropriateness of gay infantrymen is when someone asks you specifically about these things. Then, if this is the case, if I say that you think the vice president is doing a good job, I am wrong in implying that this thought or attitude is some more or less constant part of who you are. If we had some sort of science fiction mind-reading machine, we might be able to say something like "A recent survey shows that 63% of Americans think that the vice president is doing a good job, even though, according to our mind-reading machine, no one in the United States has thought about the vice president in over a year."

Two groups of people were asked how much [television] they watched a day. Both groups were given scales from which to choose. One scale started at less than thirty minutes of television a day and ended at more than two and a half hours. The other scale had a much higher minimum—less than two and a half hours—and the maximum was more than four and a half hours. In the first group, only 16.2 percent admitted to watching the greatest amount of television—more than two and a half hours. But in the second group, more than double that number said they watched at least two and a half hours. Whatever the truth, people did not want to be on the high end of the scale. (p. 23)

Most research has supported Crossen's finding that people do not want to label themselves as extremists. A 7-point scale that asks to identify people from 1 (very liberal) to 7 (very conservative) may end up, in a practical sense, as a 5-point scale because the vast majority of people will place themselves from 2 to 6. The extremes are so unstable that there is even a complex, scientific-sounding phrase—"statistical regression to the mean"—to account for the fact that if you give the same questionnaire twice to the same people, there will be fewer 1's and 7's the second time around.

The questions you ask can affect the answers that you receive. Your interest may be the public's opinion of welfare payments, but if you ask a question "Do you think welfare payments should be stopped?" you will get a different answer than if you ask "Do you think mothers and their children should receive basic support if they are unable to provide for themselves?" It is easy to be against welfare but much harder to be against mothers and their children.

In their study of the role of public opinion in the Nixon-Watergate controversy, Lang and Lang (1983) looked at two questions asked in 1973 that were used to assess the public's desire or willingness to see President Nixon impeached. The two questions were:

- If the Senate Watergate Committee decides that President Nixon was involved in the coverup, do you think Congress should impeach him, or not?
- Considering all the developments of the Watergate case, do you think Congress should begin impeachment proceedings against President Nixon, or not?

The first question is conditional: *If* Nixon was involved, *then* should he be impeached? The second question simply asks if, given what you know now, you think he should be impeached. A majority of the respondents "supported" impeachment when asked the first question, and a majority was "against" impeachment when asked the second question. Unfortunately, the wide variety of questions asked about Nixon and impeachment were all treated as indicating either support or nonsupport for impeachment, and very little care was taken by either politicians or the press to keep conclusions closely wed to the questions used to generate the data. It is easy to imagine the same sort of results if these two questions were asked regarding President Clinton.

Constructing Questions, Creating Variables

The rules for asking questions are few and clear but hard to follow in practice.

- Ask one question at a time.
- Don't ask loaded questions.
- Ask positive questions.
- Keep the questions short.

One Question at a Time

Multiple questions or complex questions are also known as "double-barreled" questions. Survey critic Cynthia Crossen (1994), a writer who should certainly know better, suggested that the question "Do you want a drug rehabilitation center in your neighborhood" be replaced with a less loaded question. The replacement she suggested was "Do you think the community needs drug rehabilitation centers, and if so, would you accept one in your neighborhood if you were persuaded that the policy process by which the locations were chosen was participatory and fair?" (pp. 118-119).

This is obviously a violation of the fourth rule ("Keep the questions short"), but it is also blatantly asking at least two questions at the same time. The first question is "Do you think the community needs drug rehabilitation centers?" The second question is "Would you accept one in your neighborhood if the location were chosen fairly?" I say "at least two questions" because the second question (which violates the rule on using neutral language) is asking (a) if you'd accept a drug rehab center and (b) if you'd accept a center if you thought the location was chosen fairly. There is very likely a group of people who do not want a drug rehabilitation center in their neighborhood no matter how the site is selected.

The second of the two questions about Nixon discussed above violates the rule about one question being asked at one time. Remember, the first question was conditional, and this conditional question is not problematic: It basically asked whether Nixon should be impeached if Congress found that he was involved in criminal activity. Regardless of what anyone thought about either Nixon or Nixon's involvement in Watergate, it was possible to answer this conditional hypothetical question. The second question, however, asked, in effect, two questions: whether you thought Nixon was involved and, if he was involved, whether you thought he should be impeached. One way to test if you are asking two questions is whether you can draw two conclusions. If you think you can conclude from the second question that people think Nixon is guilty and that they think he should be impeached, then you are asking two questions. In this case, asking the same questions of Bill Clinton would be somewhat different in that people seem to separate their thoughts about his "guilt" from their thoughts about whether he should stay in office.

Never ask about more than one thing. An even more blatant example of this, also drawn from Lang and Lang's (1983) book and involving Nixon, is "Do you think President Nixon should be impeached and compelled to leave office, or not?" Well, which one? Impeached or compelled to leave office? When developing questions, we have to look very carefully at all of our *and's* and *or's*.

Another double-barreled question is: "Do you think physicians should be able to choose their patients, or do you think that HIV-positive patients should be able to see the physician of their choice?" Like many complex questions, this one constructs a *false dilemma* suggesting that there is no way of reconciling the first half to the second half of the question. More concretely, it is possible to answer "Yes" to both halves of the question, "No" to both, or "Yes" to one and "No" to the other.

Still another double-barreled question is: "Do you think that limits should be placed on children's access to graphic pornography and violent video games?" Of course, *graphic* and *violent* are loaded terms, but the complexity of this *and* question is the same as that of the *or* question above: It is possible to feel one way about pornography and another about video games. If you can give two distinct, legitimate, noncontradictory answers to one question, then it isn't one question at all. It is two separate questions.

Loaded Questions

Loaded questions are often confused with complex questions. The problem with complex questions is that they are really two questions disguised as one. In contrast, loaded questions are questions based on an unasked assumption.

The most famous loaded question is "Have you stopped beating your wife yet?" This sounds like a yes or no question, but of course it isn't. To answer "No" means that you used to beat your wife and still do. To answer "Yes" means that you used to beat your wife but no longer do so. There is no way to answer this question if you have never beaten your wife.

Crossen's question about drug rehab centers was loaded because it assumed that there is a fair way to locate such a center rather than a number of equally unfair ways. The use of *fair* is loaded because it implies that a "no" response to the question would be unreasonable, even unethical. Look at the wording: "if you were persuaded that the process . . . was fair." What is being put to the test here is not your opinion of rehab centers but your evaluation of yourself as a fair- or unfair-minded person.

The question about *graphic* pornography and *violent* video games was also loaded. Graphic and violent by whose standards? It is difficult to be in favor of "graphic" pornography—but what if you called it "adult-oriented erotica" or "photographs depicting some nudity" or "sensuous material"?

We use loaded words in describing our positions. It makes them seem obvious and unassailable. Are you *prolife* or *prochoice?* How can anyone reasonably be against life or choice? Are you against federal *entitlement programs?* How can you be against things to which people are entitled? Are you *soft on crime?* Are you against *moral degeneracy,* or *runaway spending,* or *government intrusions?* Excuse me, but can any of this be reworded?

As a researcher, you have to avoid using terms that bias the answers you are seeking. Sometimes this is difficult, but if you think of any major social controversy or issue as something on which reasonable and good people disagree, then coming up with a reasonably neutral set of questions should not be impossible.

You should strive for neutral terminology and a reduction in the number of assumptions in any survey question.

Positive Questions

When I was a child, a man once asked me if I wanted a glass of water. I said no. "Are you sure?" he asked. "Yes," I answered, and he brought me a glass of water.

He was asking "Are you sure you *don't* want a glass of water?" and, with the mixture of positive and negative words, he confused even himself. A negative question is one that contains some negation or contradiction of the positive statement or question.

"Do you want politicians not to stop avoiding the fact that they cannot reduce the deficit without reducing their ability to successfully deny that they do not want to reduce it?"

Huh?

The best solution to the problem of negative questions is simply to avoid all negative words. This does not mean unpleasant words; it means words that make it unclear whether "Yes" means "No" or "No" means "Yes."

- *Negative:* "The government *should not stop* its fight against communism."

- *Positive:* "The government *should continue* its fight against communism."
- *Negative:* "U.S. forces should not be pulled out of Europe."
- *Positive:* "U.S. forces *should remain* in Europe" or "U.S. forces *should be pulled out* of Europe."

Short Questions

Questions in surveys, especially in face-to-face or telephone interviews, should be short. After all, you want a short answer. Crossen writes that "even if people had actually worked out a complex and sophisticated opinion," the survey format requires that they reduce it to "baby talk—yes, no, don't know" (p. 109).

More importantly, it is very difficult to follow a complex verbal statement or question. We are not a verbal society: We are a written-word society that is becoming an image society. Don't use embedded phrases, parenthetical remarks, or conditional clauses. A good rule is: Don't use commas. A better rule is: Don't use semicolons or colons. Avoid conjunctions.

Keep it short. And keep it simple.

The vocabulary used should be understood by everyone in your target population. Do not use abstract, technological, or obscure words or phrases when something simple would do just as well.

Open-Ended or Closed-Ended Questions

An *open-ended question* is one that does not supply an answer. A *close-ended* or *forced-answer* question supplies a set of answers from which the respondent gets to choose. Think of open-ended questions as either essay or short-answer test questions and forced-answer questions as multiple-choice questions.

The comparison between the two types of questions illustrates some of the validity problems associated with surveys. In studies of *media agenda setting,* researchers attempt to discover whether the mass media determine what Americans think about. This is done by looking at the topics covered by the mass media and then using a survey asking Americans to rate problems in order of importance. The agenda-setting hypothesis is supported if the survey order matches the importance given to various topics by the mass media.

Let's imagine that we have analyzed recent television news broadcasts and found that (in terms of placement and time) the most important topics covered were, in order of priority, crime, illegal immigrants, Monica Lewinsky, and political corruption. We could then ask a sample of Americans the following question:

> We want to know what you think are the major problems facing today's society.
>
> Please rank the following topics in order of importance:
>
> _____ Crime
> _____ Political corruption
> _____ Illegal immigrants
> _____ Monica Lewinsky

This guarantees that the *topics* selected as important will be the same as those used in the media; the only possible conflict will be the order of priority given to the different topics.

Another way to find out whether the public agenda matches the media agenda is to ask a question like the following:

> In order of importance, please indicate what you believe are the most important problems facing today's society.
>
> 1. _____
> 2. _____
> 3. _____
> 4. _____

The range of possible answers to this question is almost infinite. The methodological question is whether the forced-answer or the open-ended question provides the most valid measure of people's concerns. Advocates of open-ended questions argue that people should, by definition, know what their concerns are without any prompting. Advocates of close-ended questions say that given the contextless environment of survey research, it is necessary to provide choices to the respondents: People cannot be expected to rattle off major social concerns at the drop of a hat.

The benefit of close-ended questions is that they make data analysis much easier: No matter how many people you ask, you are going to have to deal with only four social problems.

A major drawback for open-ended survey questions is that the wide range of answers given will have to be reduced to be analyzed. And doing this is not easy. Should we classify an answer like "drive-by shootings" as a problem with crime, guns, gangs, youth, or something else? Are "drugs" and "the war on drugs" the same thing? Does "values in education" as an answer mean that there are not enough (of the right) values being taught, that there are too many (of the wrong values) being taught, or that no one values education anymore? If someone says that "welfare fraud" is a major problem and someone else identifies "welfare" as a major problem, can we lump these together as one variable? What about "poverty" and "homelessness"?

Once you ask people to use their own words, you face the difficulty of classifying those words into useful categories. Because survey research is a quantitative, variable-analytic methodology, it is necessary to formalize the idiosyncrasy of individual answers into a limited number of categories. The open-ended approach is very tempting—it has more face validity—but it is difficult to use. One of the techniques that I have used is to ask open-ended questions and then follow up with some forced-answer questions. This gives you a comparison to test the validity of the open-ended questions and ensures that you will have some usable data.

SCALES

One of the ways to increase the validity of a questionnaire is to ask a number of questions about any given topic rather than just one. It is difficult to reduce any interesting facet of human life to one question, and to try to do so renders the results somewhat artificial. Asking a number of questions makes it possible to draw on the complexity of an issue and to get results that are more sensitive to the nuances of opinion, belief, and perception that distinguish us.

When studying perceptions of AIDS, my research team (under the direction of Dr. Barbara Gerbert) knew that there were different levels of knowledge about the disease and that it would not be possible to ask one question to determine how knowledgeable people were. We went through the existing research and pulled together a number of questions that had been used to measure AIDS knowledge and formed them into a scale. The results looked like this (a partial list):

On a scale from *very likely* to *very unlikely,* how likely do you think it is that someone could contract AIDS in the following situations? (Circle the appropriate response.)

1. Donating or giving blood

very likely	somewhat likely	somewhat unlikely	very unlikely	definitely not possible
1	2	3	4	5

2. Having sex with a person who has the AIDS virus

very likely	somewhat likely	somewhat unlikely	very unlikely	definitely not possible
1	2	3	4	5

3. Eating in a restaurant where the cook has the AIDS virus

very likely	somewhat likely	somewhat unlikely	very unlikely	definitely not possible
1	2	3	4	5

The actual scale consisted of nine items, but this shorter list is sufficient to illustrate scale construction. We want to add these variables together to form a new variable—a *scaled* variable—called *KNOW.*

To create KNOW, we need to look at the *direction* the variables take. To find the direction of the variables, you have to under-

Table 8.1 A Data Sheet With Scaled Data

Variables	Respondents									
	1	*2*	*3*	*4*	*5*	*6*	*7*	*8*	*9*	*10*
Variable 1	1	2	1	4	2	3	4	3	2	4
Variable 2	1	3	3	4	5	3	5	2	2	5
Variable 3	1	3	1	4	4	3	5	2	3	3
KNOW	3	8	5	12	11	9	14	7	7	12

stand what is indicated by the scores on each item. In the first variable, saying that donating blood is very or somewhat likely to lead to AIDS shows that the respondent does not understand how AIDS is contracted. So for this variable a low numerical score indicates low knowledge of AIDS. In the second variable, a low numerical score *indicates knowledge* of AIDS because having sex with someone who is infected with HIV *is* one of the ways of becoming infected. The third variable is like the first in that, because this *is not* a known way of getting infected, a low number indicates low knowledge.

Because it makes sense to think of high numbers as indicating more knowledge, we will want to reverse the scores on the second variable, the one about sex. Using a computer, this is fairly easy to do: You turn all the 1's into 5's, 2's into 4's, 3's into 2's, 2's into 3's, and so on. This allows you to add up the variables so that the bigger the number, the greater the knowledge.

Now, rather than three variables that each have a *range* from 1 to 5, we now have a new variable, KNOW, with a range from 3 to 15. This greater range allows us to make finer distinctions, which can result in greater validity (Table 8.1).

This creation of scales also allows us to make more fine-tuned comparisons. For example, let's imagine that all the even-numbered respondents in the table above were men and that all the odd-numbered respondents were women. The overall *mean* (average) for the variable KNOW is 8.8 (3 + 8 + 5 + 12 + 11 + 9 + 14 + 7 + 7 + 12 = 88, and 88 divided by 10 is 8.8). The mean score for men is 9.6, and the mean score for women is 8.0. If your hypothesis was that men would be more knowledgeable about AIDS because it disproportionately affects men, then this sort of data would provide support.

Scales can also have *dimensions.* We can imagine a scale that consists of 20 questions designed to find out where people are on a scale from "very conservative" to "very liberal." We recognize that ideological beliefs are very complex things (which is why a scale is more meaningful than a dichotomous variable), so within our 20-item scale we will have items that get at various aspects (or dimensions) of political belief. We could have, for example, five questions about economics, five about personal freedoms, five about international relations, and five about "morality." These "dimensions" are subscales within the larger scale about political beliefs.

DATA COLLECTION

Although the most common way of gathering survey data is the telephone interview, it is not the only way. Survey data can also be gathered in face-to-face interviews and through mailed questionnaires. Each of these methods has its advantages and disadvantages.

Telephone Interviews

Telephone interviewing has a number of advantages: It is relatively inexpensive, it is comparatively fast, it is very amenable to random sampling techniques, it is safe, and it can be computer-driven. Its drawbacks are that the questions must be kept very simple and that the credibility of the telephone interviewer has been seriously undermined by telemarketers.

Telephone survey research is relatively inexpensive in that *if your telephone system is set up in such a way that only completed calls are billed,* then you do not have to pay for nonresponses. Many commercial telephone accounts allow you to hang up as soon as you hear an answering machine without the call being billed as a completed connection. Compare this to a mail survey in which the cost of a nonresponse is almost equal to that of a response. You can see the relative advantages of the telephone.

Further, because telephone data collection avoids the lag time of mail surveys or the collection time of face-to-face data collection, it is by far the fastest way to collect data. This is why political pollsters use telephone surveys.

Sampling techniques in telephone surveys are either equal or superior to those used in mail surveys. The designs are equal when using purchased data lists or in-house lists (of customers, clients, or members) and superior if you are using a random-digit-dialing sampling design. Random-digit dialing is a technique used in Computer-Assisted Telephone Interviewing (or CATI). With a CATI system, you set the program to randomly select (and dial) telephone numbers—and you can preset the parameters of the randomness. For example, if you wanted a random sample of Americans, the program could generate 10-digit phone numbers (area code + prefix + local extension), or you could select the area codes you were interested in and have the program generate local extensions.

By being plugged directly into a computer, CATI interviewing allows the interviewer to input data directly into the computer. This avoids the two-step limitation of mail surveys (first on paper, then inputted into the computer): The more steps you have in data collection/entry, the more places you have for mistakes to creep into the process. Some face-to-face surveys are now conducted using small, hand-held computers, which provide a similar advantage.

Telephone interviewers have to be trained. The problem is that interviewers can bias the answers they receive. This means not only that interviewers can cheat (as they occasionally do) but that they can "help" respondents choose an answer. There is a fine line between helping and *prompting,* and interviewers must be trained not to cross this line. *Prompts* are *scripted remarks* that interviewers use to get respondents to answer:

> Interviewer: Do you strongly agree, somewhat agree, neither agree nor disagree, somewhat disagree, or disagree strongly with the remark that Congress should be abolished?
> Respondent: Uhhh. . . .
> Interviewer: Would you like me to repeat the question?
> Respondent: No, it's just that . . . uhhh. . . .
> Interviewer: Do you basically agree or disagree with this remark?
> Respondent: Agree, I guess.
> Interviewer: Would you say that you strongly agree or only somewhat agree with this remark?
> Respondent: Somewhat, I think.
> Interviewer: Ok. The next question is. . . .

The interviewer helps the respondent without biasing the results. If, at the end of this interchange, the respondent says that he or she "strongly agrees" that Congress should be abolished, then the interviewer must simply record the answer and not blurt out that people should not need to be prompted about something they feel strongly about. An inappropriate form of prompting is one that adds new information to the question, making it different than the question answered by other respondents:

> Interviewer: Do you strongly agree, somewhat agree, neither agree nor disagree, somewhat disagree, or disagree strongly with the remark that Congress should be abolished?
> Respondent: Uhhh. . . .
> Interviewer: You know, do you think Congress spends too much of our money, or is too political, or do you think they're doing a good job?

Mail Surveys

Mail surveys, in comparison, require little training. Every respondent receives exactly the same questions. If the questions are all closed-ended, then data entry (the transferring of the information from the questionnaires to the computer) is also straightforward, requiring few, if any, judgment calls.

The disadvantages of mail surveys are the cost of nonrespondents and the turnaround time of questionnaires. It usually takes less than a minute to find out if a person in a telephone interview is going to respond or not—so the cost of nonrespondents is very low. In contrast, the cost of *mailing* a questionnaire to a nonrespondent is identical to the cost of sending one to a person who actually completes it. In both cases, the researcher has to pay for printing, stationery, and outgoing postage. The only added expense for respondents is the cost of return mail. And even this added expense has to be balanced against the cost of a second mailing. In mail surveys, it is always a good idea to do a second mailing to the people who did not respond to the first mailing. The end result of this, however, is that nonrespondents in mail surveys cost you more than respondents.

Turnaround time is also a problem. You can expect a gap of about a week between the time of mailing and the time when the questionnaires start coming back in. Generally, it is a good idea to wait at least 2 weeks before doing a second mailing. Given that the second mailing will also take about 2 weeks to complete, the total time involved in data collection is at least a month. Quite often this time lag does not present a problem. However, as mentioned above, the longer you spend collecting your data, the more likely it is that time will become a relevant variable (Table 8.2).

Face-to-Face Interviews

The variety of face-to-face interview techniques makes it difficult to generalize about this method of data collection. One face-to-face interviewing technique is *intercept* research. Intercept

Table 8.2 Survey Data Collection Comparisons

	Mail	Face to Face	Telephone
Cost	High	Very high	Low
Speed	Moderate	Very slow	Fast
Safety	Safe	Possibly dangerous	Safe
Sampling	Good	Difficult	Good
Data control	Good	Difficult	Very good
Training	None	Difficult	Difficult

research, as the name implies, is a technique in which the interviewer stops (or *intercepts*) people to ask them questions. This type of research is frequently done in public places, such as malls, resort areas, and amusement parks, and is used in market research. The advantage of this technique is that you can directly reach the population in which you are interested. The disadvantage is that the interviews have to be fairly short and it is difficult to establish a sampling design. This type of research is moving away from the clipboard-and-paper approach to the use of hand-held computers, a move that improves data management and control.

Face-to-face interviews, like telephone interviews, require a well-trained staff of interceptors. The more contact an interviewer has with a respondent, the greater the opportunity to bias the results.

Another form of face-to-face data collection is the door-to-door type. With this type of research, the sample design usually is structured around addresses or neighborhoods. One of the advantages of this approach is that the response rate tends to be high: It is more difficult to close a door in someone's face than to throw away a letter or hang up a phone. This type of data collection is also useful when trying to interview people who do not have telephones or are unlikely to show up on commercial mailing or telephone lists.

The disadvantages of door-to-door research are that it is dangerous, slow, and expensive. It is always more dangerous to deal with people in person than over the telephone or through the mail. This is even more the case when the interviews are taking place in the respondent's territory. One of the reasons that this sort of interviewing is expensive is that it is prudent to send out interviewers in pairs to reduce the danger.

Another reason why it is expensive is simply that it takes longer to walk from house to house than to dial a number or to drop a bundle of questionnaires in the mail. This means that labor costs are quite high.

SAMPLING FOR SURVEYS

We have seen that sampling is critical in all forms of research. In fieldwork and experimental research, however, the methodologies themselves limit the researcher's ability to really concentrate on sampling. In fieldwork, sampling is generally limited to time and place. "Snowball" sampling is also used in fieldwork. Snowball sampling is a crude form of sampling in which the researcher asks each person interviewed if he or she could provide the name of another person willing to be interviewed. If you think about this, you can see how the sample could get seriously skewed. Imagine that I ask you to give me the names of one or two other students and then ask each of those students to each name one or two additional students. I could get a fair number of people this way, but it would be questionable if they represented anything other than one of the social strata on the campus.

One of the problems with fieldwork is that there is a minimum of *data reduction*—fieldwork is not *variable analytic,* as you remember—which means that it is difficult to summarize the data. This means that there is a limit, and a rather low limit, to the number of subjects you can study. The same thing is also true of experiments. This is not because experiments are not variable analytic (experiments are *always* variable analytic) but because experiments are difficult to conduct with large numbers of people.

In contrast to fieldwork and experimental research, with survey research one can study hundreds, if not thousands, of people with relative ease. This ability to have large samples allows the researcher to make finer distinctions between subjects than is generally possible with research that uses smaller samples. With smaller samples, the researcher is forced to ignore a great many social and demographic variables as irrelevant. This is one of the reasons that in experiments one must ask one question at a time. In survey research, it is possible to make a fairly large number of contrasts with relatively little effort.

Types of Sampling Designs

You'll remember from Chapter 4 that there were two basic types of sampling designs: probability and nonprobability sampling. Probability sampling includes both systematic and random sampling designs. Nonprobability sampling involves convenience sampling and sampling of extremely low numbers of subjects. This difference is very important in survey research.

The key to probability sampling is that everyone in a target population (i.e., the group about which you wish to generalize) has an equal chance of being included in the sample. This is why *random sampling* is superior to *systematic sampling:* In systematic sampling, one chooses every Nth person, which means that every non-Nth person has no chance of being selected to be part of the sample. Imagine that you want to talk about students at Cal State Stanislaus. There are 5,800 students enrolled, and you want to select a sample of 500. You divide 5,800 by 500, which gives you 11.6, which you round down to 11. (If you rounded up to 12, you would only get 483 people in your sample. It is better to get slightly more than too few.) This means that you include every 11th student in your sample. And this means that each time you pick a person, the following 10 people have no chance of being included in the sample. In comparison, if you are randomly choosing 500, then every one of the 5,800 students has an equal chance of being included. Systematic samples are good—it's just that random samples are better. They are *cleaner* from the perspective of pure probability.

Why would you choose to do systematic rather than random sampling? It usually depends on the *sampling frame.* The sampling frame is the source of your sample. In the example above, it could be the list of students at the Office of Admissions and Records. If it is possible to get a list, then it is possible to do random sampling. If the list is computerized, it is usually possible for the computer to randomly select a sample. If the list is printed, as in a telephone book, it is possible to select pages randomly using a random number table and then to use another random number table to select names from each page.

But usually, with something as bulky as a telephone book, it is easier to use systematic sampling. If the phone book has 1,234 pages and you want a sample of 500, you divide 1,234 by 500 to get 2.46. This number, 2.46, means you have to look at every two and a half pages. Because looking at a half-page makes no sense, you can choose to look at every second page (rounding down) or every third page (rounding up). Rounding down means you won't finish the book. (Two times 500 equals 1,000 and the phone book is 1,234 pages thick. This means, for example, that you're excluding all the Zanaeckis from your sample.) Rounding up means you'll finish the book before you complete your sample (three times 500 equals 1,500). In this case, I would look at page 2, then page 5, then page 7, then page 10: a *second* page, then a *third* page then a *second* page, and so on. This is not nuclear physics: The point is to produce a sample in which everyone in the population has an known, equal chance of participating. In this case, that simply means that pages throughout the phone book will be selected.

And how do you select the names from each page? Systematically, of course. You could take the first name on the first selected page, the second name on the second selected page, and continue until you have reached the last name on the page and then start again at the first name. Or you could skip names: the first name on the first selected page, the third name on the second selected page, and so on.

Sampling gets more complicated if there is no one list that names the members of the population that one wants to sample. Imagine, for example, that one wants to study members of churches in Stanislaus County. There are two ways to sample for this study. The researcher could, using the telephone book or a random-digit-dialing computer program, randomly or systematically sample everyone in Stanislaus County and ask each respondent if he or she is a member of a church. Only those who claim such membership would be included in the sample. This is notoriously unreliable because people will identify themselves as members of churches with which they have no affiliation. Studies that have been conducted in this way show that church membership and attendance greatly exceed the available capacity.

Because of this, a better way to reach church members is to go to churches and get their lists of members. Now, the problem here is this: Our unit of analysis is individual members, but our sampling frame consists of churches. There are approximately 380 churches in Stanislaus County, with memberships ranging from a few dozen to a few thousand adult members. Because of the variation in size, we cannot treat each church as we can treat each page in a phone book. Let's imagine we want to draw a sample of 1,000 church members. If we treat each church the same as all other churches, then we could divide 1,000 by 380, which would mean that we would have to contact slightly more than two and a half people per church. (Here, of course, we would round up to three because interviewing a half-person is a tricky business.)

This is not a good sampling design. Remember what the *unit of analysis* is. We are not trying to survey *churches,* we are trying to survey a representative sample of county churchgoers. This means that if you are a member of the 5,000- member Big County Church you should have a greater chance of being selected as part of the sample than a member of the 4-member First Church of

Table 8.3 An Example of Stratified Sampling

Name of Church	Membership	Percentage
Big County Church	17,500	25%
Small County Church	3,500	5%
First Church of God	7,000	10%
Third Church of God	3,500	5%
City Temple	3,500	5%
Church of Conservative Politics	21,000	30%
St. Somebody	7,000	10%
Church of Liberal Social Policies	7,000	10%
Total population of churchgoers	70,000	100%

Home Worship or the 15-member Turlock Coven of Witches and Warlocks.

Just to make life easier, let's imagine that there are only eight churches in the county and we still want to get a sample of 1,000 churchgoers. Table 8.3 shows a list of the churches and their memberships.

Now, if we were to do a *stratified sampling* of this population, we would want a sample that contained 250 members of the Big County Church, 100 members of the Small County Church, and so on. We would want 250 members of Big County because members of that church make up 25% of the churchgoing population and 250 is 25% of a sample of 1,000. This would be the easiest way of sampling this population, given the availability of church membership lists. All we would have to do would be to *randomly or systematically* select the appropriate number of people from each list.

A more complicated way of doing this would be to dump all the names into one list but to *weigh* them differently so that a member of Big County would have a 1 in 4 chance of being selected (25% means one out of four churchgoers), whereas members of the Church of Liberal Social Policies would have a only 1 in 10 chance of being selected. This sort of weighed sampling is known as *sampling proportionate to size.*

An important point to keep in mind is that if your sample size is large enough, then stratified sampling is unnecessary. This is because the results of a random sample, if the size is sufficient, will look pretty much like the population from which it is drawn. One of the reasons, then, for using a stratified sample is that you lack the resources to conduct a large enough random sample.

RESPONSE RATES

One of the problems with sample designs is that they may not work out in reality. Imagine all the people you would invite to your house if you wanted to have the perfect party—your favorite writers and celebrities as well as your friends—then imagine how many of them would actually show up. The difference between those "invited" to participate in a survey and those who actually "show up" to participate is known as the response rate.

Response rates are very important. Unfortunately, it is possible to become obsessed with them and to believe that a response rate of 60% is acceptable whereas a response rate of 58% is not. Quite often in sampling, people become overly rule bound. They lose track of *why* response rates are important and think that the rates themselves are somehow magical.

Let's imagine that you want to conduct a telephone survey of Californians. Your goal is to have 1,200 respondents, and you are going to use random-digit dialing. By the time you have completed 1,200 interviews, you have dialed 2,625 numbers. The breakdown is shown in Table 8.4.

There are a number of ways of calculating a response rate. The most obvious is to divide the number of completed interviews by the total number of phone numbers dialed (letters sent, people intercepted, etc.). In this case, that means you divide 1,200 by 2,625. This gives you a response rate of 45%. But because you were trying to talk to Californians and *not* to California busi-

Table 8.4 Calculating Response Rates

Type of Contact	Numbers
Completed interviews	1,200
Disconnected numbers	163
Refusals	74
Businesses	475
Fax machines and computers	87
No answers or answering machines	434
Respondents do not speak English	192
Total numbers dialed	2,625

nesses, you will probably want to drop those 475 dials from the total. The same is true for answering machines and disconnects ("I'm sorry, but the number you have dialed is no longer a working number"). This means you divide the number of completed interviews by the number of *possible* interviews (or "valid numbers"), or, in this case, 1,200 by 1,987. This gives you a response rate of 60%.

Even that figure—1,987—is a little biased. After all, the phone may go unanswered because the person who is supposed to answer it is dead. (Lang and Lang, 1983, found that a goodly proportion of registered voters who didn't vote were dead rather than lazy.) And if 18% (475 divided by 2,551) of all the numbers dialed were businesses, can we assume that *some* significant percentage of the unanswered phones were businesses? Or non-English speakers?

So calculating the response rate requires some creativity. But let's accept the 60% response rate as legitimate. By almost everyone's standards, a response rate this high is quite acceptable. The sample, however, can still be bad.

Telephone surveys conducted primarily during the day result in respondents who are disproportionately female, elderly, and poor. That would make a bad sample of Californians regardless

of the response rate. On the other hand, you could have a low response rate—say, 25%—and have a sample that looked pretty
much like California in terms of age, ethnicity, income, and sex.
In this case, rejecting the sample because of the response rate
would make no sense. Research has shown that there really are no
significant differences between those who respond and those who
do not, but there is a difference between those who are home during the day and those who are not.

A sample is biased or inadequate when it is possible to state a
reason why those in the sample cannot be used to represent the
population. There is no magic number that guarantees that a
sample is good. A 100% response rate on a bad design will result
in a bad sample.

The best way to improve your response rate is to recontact the
nonrespondents. If a phone is unanswered, call back at a different
time and on a different day. People tend to be at home and away
from home in patterns, so it makes little sense to continue calling
at the same time. As part of your design, plan to call back a certain number of times (three, four, or five). If you are conducting a
mail survey, remail to nonrespondents at least once or twice.

EU NAO FALO INGLES

What does it mean to survey *Californians?* One thing for sure—it
means that you will speak to a lot of people who are not native
English speakers. The title for this section says "I don't speak
English" in Portuguese. Doing telephone interviewing, you will
encounter all levels of English language ability, from no English
at all to English fluency.

And if Californians do not speak English, what do they speak?
Virtually everything. Spanish, of course, is a major language in
California, as is Chinese (both Mandarin and Cantonese), but
there are dozens of languages and dialects spoken.

What should a researcher do with non- or poor English speakers? On a purely pragmatic basis, it must be recognized that it is

not possible to have a staff capable of handling every language that one encounters. Given that, what must one do?

You need to have bilingual interviewers in the major languages in the area being surveyed. You need to have questionnaires in English, Spanish, and Chinese.

If you cannot speak the language of the person answering the phone (or the door), then have that person recontacted by someone who *does* speak the language. Another option is to recontact at a different time. Quite often, someone in the house speaks English. Unfortunately, that is usually the person who is least likely to be home.

One more thing to keep in mind with doing research that includes non-English speakers: There are cultural and experiential barriers over and above the linguistic ones. Non-English speakers tend, obviously enough, to be immigrants, and they may not come from societies or cultures in which one freely gives information to strangers over the phone. Social scientists ask questions about sexual practices, religious beliefs, family structures, political opinions, occupational perceptions, and other things that may be considered as too private or too dangerous to discuss openly with strangers on the phone.

CONFIDENTIALITY AND ANONYMITY

Remember: If a survey is *confidential,* then the researcher knows who the respondent is. If the survey is conducted *anonymously,* then the researcher does not know who the respondent is. Oddly enough, anonymity is more likely in some forms of face-to-face interviews than in either mail or telephone surveys. This is because if one is doing intercepts, one does not have to keep track of potential respondents.

If one is sampling by telephone number or by address (either mail or in person), then one has to keep track of those who respond in order to keep track of those who do not. In mail surveys, researchers usually survey in at least two waves. In telephone sur-

To ensure confidentiality, please return this postcard. Do not mail it in the survey envelope. Do not put your name on the survey.

Please check one of the boxes below.

❏ I completed and returned the survey

❏ I do not want to participate in this survey.

If you have any questions about this survey or about its confidentiality, please contact Dr. Joseph Blow at 555-6754. Or write to the address on the front of this postcard.

We would like to thank you for your time.

Figure 8.1. Sample Postcard

veys, researchers generally call back numerous times to reach people who do not initially answer their phones.

In Mail Surveys

This means that on a mail survey, there has to be some way of tracking respondents. One way that I use is the postcard method. In this method, the survey goes out to all the respondents and contains a cover letter, a survey form, a stamped return envelope, and a stamped return postcard. The postcard has the person's name on it, whereas the survey instrument does not. The postcard allows us to cross off those who respond in the first wave so that they are not included in the second wave (Figure 8.1).

Table 8.5 Sample Telephone Code Sheet, Generated Each Day

Phone #	Time	Day	Response	Codes		
5554409	3	m	A	Time		
5554443	3	m	A		1	Morning
5554477	3	m	L		2	Afternoon
5554511	3	m	NA		3	Evening
5554545	3	m	NA			
5554579	3	m	B	Day		
5554613	3	m	NA		m	Monday
5554647	3	m	A		t	Tuesday
5554681	3	m	R		w	Wednesday
5554715	3	m	R		r	Thursday
5554749	3	m	NA		f	Friday
5554783	3	m	B		s	Saturday
5554817	3	m	A			
5554851	3	m	A	Response		
5554885	3	m	L		NA	No answer (includes answering machines)
5554919	3	m	NA		L	Language other than English (specify for callback)
5554953	3	m	B		B	Busy
5554987	3	m	R		NR	Nonresidential (business, fax, disconnects, etc.)
5555021	3	m	R		CB	request for callback
5555055	3	m	R		A	Answer, completes survey
5555089	3	m	A		R	Refusal
5555123	3	m	R			

In Telephone Surveys

In telephone interviewing, the procedure is much simpler. In this method, the interviewer is using a master list that is either printed out or on the computer screen. In either case, the interviewer keeps track of phone calls as they are made. The code sheet in Table 8.5 shows how researchers abbreviate the responses so that the code sheets can be easily sorted for the next shift. Note that the interviewer indicates the time of day and the day of the week that the call was made. This is so that callbacks can be made at different times, in the hope of reaching as many people as possible.

A similar code sheet can be developed for door-to-door interviewing.

With all of this types of interviewing, the researcher *never* puts *any* codes or marks on the survey that would allow the respondent to be identified. Pretest-posttest designs require you to bend this rule somewhat. When you are using a survey as a pretest/posttest, you will have to be able to identify all tests so that they can be matched in pairs. To do this, you should give each respondent a randomly generated code number that is kept in a secure place for the duration of the experiment. Once the pretests and posttests have been matched, the file linking the code numbers to any person should be destroyed.[1]

HINTS FOR DEVELOPING A QUESTIONNAIRE

First, never ask whether people agree or disagree with a *question.* For example:

Do you think that the Kenneth Starr report should have been on the Internet?

1	2	3	4	5
strongly agree	agree	undecided	disagree	strongly disagree

This is a common mistake for people developing a questionnaire for the first time. It is *not possible* to agree with a question.

Second, don't use technical or academic words unless it is absolutely necessary. The use of such words can bias the results and can create misunderstanding. Some examples from student papers are listed and discussed next.

How many days do you drink alcohol out of the week?

The word *alcohol* is very clinical and negative. It is also misleading in that people do not drink *alcohol,* they drink beverages
that have alcohol in them. Ask people what you want to know,
and ask them directly, in ordinary language: "How many days a
week do you have a glass of wine, a beer, or a drink with liquor in
it?" "Having a beer" sounds less diabolically self-destructive
than "drinking alcohol." Asking how often one drinks *alcohol* is
like asking how often one drinks *chemicals.*

After cohabitation, I would expect to be married.

People only "cohabitate" in social science journal articles. In
real life, they live together. Because of this, you should ask if they
live together. "Living together" sounds less technical than cohabitation. It also sounds less judgmental. In your write-up, you can
refer to it as cohabitation, if that is how your audience is used to
thinking about it, but not in your survey.

Respond to the following situations by using one of the following responses: AS (assertively), AG (aggressively), NA (non-
assertively).

The distinction between *aggressive* behavior and *assertive*
behavior is clear to anyone who has taken a course based in interpersonal communication theories or research. The distinction,
however, is entirely academic. That is, communication scholars
want to distinguish between what they consider to be *good* active
responses and *bad* active responses, so they have defined the two
words in this way. In nonacademic speech, the distinction between the two words is much less clear, and you cannot assume
that the ordinary person will use the words in any academically
correct fashion.

In this case, in which a situation is defined and you want to
know how a person would behave, you should define three forms

of behavior that academics would recognize as assertive, aggressive, and passive. Let the respondents choose between the forms
of behavior: "I'd politely and firmly tell him that he is wrong"; "I
would wring his chicken neck"; "I'd agree with him because it
isn't worth getting fired."

Third, in a face-to-face or a phone survey, do not ask for a person's sex. Men and women like to think that it is obvious that they
are men and women. Imagine someone looking right at you and
asking if you are a man or a woman—a little weird, eh? If you are
on the phone and really cannot tell the sex of the person with
whom you are speaking, wait until you have finished with all of
your questions and then ask for age and sex together. Introduce it
with some throwaway line such as "and now I have to ask a couple of bureaucratic questions. . . ."

Fourth, ask questions about income at the end of the survey. Income questions are sensitive and can result in people hanging up
or throwing away a mail survey. If you put such questions at the
end, the person has already invested so much time that he or she is
unlikely to throw it all away.

Last, when using a scale, use an odd number of choices to allow
for a neutral answer. Scales with either five or seven items are
most common.

WRITING

The most common problem I have found in student papers that
use survey research is that variables are not operationalized very
clearly. Sometimes the problem is that although the student's
variables are well operationalized it is not at all clear how the related variables in previous research have been operationalized.
For example, if you are studying violence on television, let the
reader know not only how you operationalized the key terms but
how your operationalizations relate to those used by other researchers in this area. One study could find a great deal of vio-

lence and another very little when the primary difference is the operationalizations used.

COMMENTS

Ethical Issues

Surveys tend not to raise a great many ethical issues. The subjects have a lot of control, survey research is not manipulative, and the methodology lends itself easily to anonymity and confidentiality.

In this methodology, there is a significant overlap between *ethically questionable* research and *methodologically questionable* research. Deliberately biasing questions, for example, raises both ethical and research issues. *Push-pull* research in which surveys are used to create attitudes is also simultaneously methodologically and ethically bad. Push-pull research is used in political and marketing research to change people's opinions and to benefit from that change. Asking people extensive questions about fear and crime and then asking if they know that the Acme Alarm Company has created peace of mind among some of their neighbors is an example of push-pull research. The George W. Bush primary campaign in South Carolina was accused of using push-pull tactics against John McCain by asking those who said they supported McCain if they did so despite a number of negative factors, which they then enumerated.

Connections

As mentioned in the previous chapter, survey-type questionnaires are often used in experimental research.

Survey research can make use of open-ended questions, and when it does so the researcher can find him- or herself doing content analysis. When this is the case, be as open as possible in

---

SIDEBAR 8.3 Vocabulary

Attrition	CATI	cohort study
Cross-sectional	Dimensions	False dilemma
Forced-answer	Intercepts	Loaded questions
Longitudinal	Open-ended	Panel study
Prompts	Random-digit dialing	Response rate
Sampling frame	Socially preferred answers	

---

describing how the large number of open-ended remarks were reduced to the generalized statements included in the write-up.

ACTIVITIES AND EXERCISES

1. You are interested in the impact of high school experience on people's lives. You decide that a survey is the most appropriate methodology. How would you design the study?

2. There is a great deal of talk about "family values" and "traditional values" and their connection to social and political beliefs and behaviors. Using survey methodology, how would you go about studying this connection?

NOTE

1. It always makes a researcher uneasy to destroy any kind of data. You may be tempted to keep a copy of the codes linking pretest and posttest, but there really is no reason. Matching numbers on the paper copies would be enough should you ever have to reenter the data due to file corruption of some sort. I always keep a master file (which I label MASTER) and run all my statistical analyses on a work file (which I label WORK).

9

CONTENT ANALYSIS

So far, we have been looking at ways to study people in a more or less direct fashion. In fieldwork we have watched people in natural settings, and in experiments we have investigated the way people behave in contrived situations. In surveys we have asked people questions to determine their knowledge, attitudes, and beliefs. But in this book we are focusing on communication research, and because an increasingly large portion of our communication is preserved (or preservable), we have a way to study people *indirectly.*

We leave tracks, so to speak, as we work our way through life: videotapes, memos, letters, films and television programs, books, newspapers, magazines, e-mail messages, check stubs, popular music, and music videos. These are like frozen bits of communication and behavior that can be analyzed to learn about who we are, what we think and believe, what we value, and what we do.

For the most part, content analysis research centers on the mass media. In a society such as ours, which is saturated with commercially produced cultural products, the world presented via the media is the only one most of us know. Because of this, it is important to understand the sorts of messages that the media produce. Questions concerning *why* the media produce what they do and what impact the media has on the audience are questions that *cannot* be answered by studying media content. Content analysis is capable only of discussing content.

For purposes of simplicity, anything that can be analyzed will be called a text. In this special sense of the word, we can call song lyrics, video presentations, novels, and virtually anything else *texts.*

MANIFEST AND LATENT CONTENT

The *manifest* content is the surface meaning of a message. The *latent* content is the underlying meaning or implications of the message. The latent content is always more disputable than the manifest content. In this sense, latent content is like *nonverbal communication:* We know it means something, but the meaning is ambiguous. Or it is like political analysis: We know what it means to say that the Federal Reserve Bank has raised interest rates (manifest content), but what this means for the economy is open to interpretation (latent content).

Imagine that you are in a meeting with a number of people and your supervisor turns to you and says, "Why don't you go get us some coffee?"

The manifest meaning of the remark is that your supervisor wants you to go get some coffee. The possible latent meanings are endless and require an understanding of the context in which the remark was made. The first questions, of course, are why *you* and why *now?* The implication, the *latent meaning,* is that you are the most dispensable person in the meeting. Another meaning of the remark is that your supervisor has the power to make you do things you may not want to do. Suppose you had just interjected a new idea into the discussion and then your supervisor immediately responded by asking you to get some coffee. The meaning of the remark could simply be that power was being asserted; in this sense, there would be no difference between saying any of the fol-

SIDEBAR 9.1 You've Come a Long Way—Maybe

Television commercials package women's beauty products as sources of power. The *manifest* message of these commercials is that women can control their appearance and can form themselves into the kinds of women they want to be through the use of various chemicals, dyes, scents, and elastic. The very process of aging can now be brought under control with hair dyes and wrinkle cream.

These messages of empowerment tend to depict women as independent, powerful, on the go, happy, satisfied, and loved. But what is the latent message?

The latent message is that the value of a woman is in her appearance. No gray, no wrinkles, no fat, no evidence of work or childbearing is allowed. It is a strange sort of empowerment that reduces people to their appearance.

In contrast, men are defined by their actions, and their actions are usually of two types: buying things and jumping off things. The images of both men and women in commercial culture are one-dimensional and fairly pathetic, but for one sex they are action oriented and for the other they are appearance based.

lowing: "Why don't you go get us some coffee?" "Why don't you go get us some cookies?" "Why don't you let me do the talking?"

In this same sense, we can look at the horror movies of the 1950s and see that although the manifest content is about heroic Americans fighting alien dangers, the latent content is more plausibly about American fears of communism and Americans' tremendously ambivalent attitudes about conformity. In the same way, a look at television crime shows indicates a latent meaning that is strongly conservative. In this way, fictional crime shows are much like news in that on the surface they may have certain liberal postures but these postures are acted out on a solidly conservative base in which traditionally defined values are rewarded and traditionally defined sins are punished.

SIDEBAR 9.2 Sex on Television: Operationalization

If we want to study sex on television, nudity certainly seems like a good way to operationalize it. But consider the following example:

In an episode of the television program *Chicago Hope*, an extremely attractive 17-year-old girl has a tumor removed from her breast. The story focuses on the girl's reaction to the thought of having her breast removed. It turns out the tumor is not malignant, so the breast is not removed, but the nipple has to be reconstructed by a plastic surgeon.

The final scene shows the girl looking at her breasts, saved by the miracles of modern medicine. The camera shows the girl's breasts as she lies in her hospital bed, surrounded by her doctors and her mother. As far as I know, this is the first instance of this type of nudity on television. The question is whether or not this is "sexy." Are women's breasts sex objects no matter what the context? The answer is "simply" a matter of how one operationalizes the idea of "sex" or "sexiness."

To operationalize a concept is to say how you will determine which attribute applies to each unit in your sample. This example indicates how difficult this is. Nudity can be used for many things besides titillation. It can be used as humor, as tragedy, as biology, and as all of these in some combination.

Content analysis attempts to get at the latent meanings of texts or to contrast the latent and manifest meanings. Many times it is this contrast that is interesting. Take, for example, the television situation comedy *My Two Dads.* This is one of the many programs that modify the traditional family setting used in situation comedies. Because there are two "dads" rather than a father and a mother, this program seems to embody liberal values of experimentation, open-mindedness, and flexibility in values. That is the manifest level of meaning. Any viewing of this or similar network programs will reveal, however, that the basic moral messages around which each episode is constructed are very traditional. At this latent level, the programs are very conservative: Be fair, be individualistic, hard work pays off, family comes first, people get what they deserve. This latent message is the same whether the family is a traditional white suburban family (*Seventh Heaven, Growing Pains, Family Ties*), a minority family (*The Cosby Show, Family Matters*), a collective (*Full House*), a single-parent family (*Buffy, Who's the Boss, Phenom*), or simply strange (*My Two Dads, Sister Sister, Sabrina*).

Because latent meaning is, by definition, not obvious, it runs the risk of sounding contrived: Aliens are really communists, "liberal" programs are actually "conservative." Because of this, any efforts to argue for a latent meaning must be very persuasive, bringing in a great deal of context, negating alternative explanations, and providing as much data as possible.

It may be helpful to think of meaning as occurring at three different levels or as three different types. Many theorists have recognized that more than one form of meaning can be applicable to a single message. I have conceptualized meaning as having the following levels:

- *Facts:* the parts of a message or event that can be evaluated as either true or false
- *Explanations:* the parts of a message that attempt to relate two or more things in a causal manner
- *Interpretations:* the importance or ramifications of a message or event

My research has shown, not surprisingly, that as one moves down this typology, there is more and more disagreement. Looking at the news, viewers who think that six cars were involved in a pile-up after it was reported that five cars were involved have made a mistake. Their belief that six cars were involved is false. This is the level of facts. But most news stories go beyond the level of facts, and in this case we could imagine the newscaster attributing the accident to rain and wet roads. This is the level of explanation. At the level of explanation, you can think something different from what is contained in the story and yet not be wrong. You know that it has in fact been raining, for example, but you still may think that driver stupidity or careless-ness was a more probable cause. After all, many people drive in the rain, and only a tiny fraction get involved in accidents. So, you reason, rain, by itself, cannot be the cause. This is a matter of debate: It is different from thinking that six cars were involved in the five-car pile-up. You have to concede that rain makes driving more hazardous, and the newscasters have to concede that rain, by itself, does not cause accidents. The level of certainty in expla-nations is always less than it is for facts.

Finally, there is the level of interpretation or importance. You may think that this accident is horrific and may be unable to sleep for days. Other people many not be overly concerned. Some peo-ple may know the victims, and then this accident could be a turn-ing point in their lives. This is the level of interpretation, and here meaning becomes very personal—based on knowledge, expe-rience, salience, values, ideologies, social position, and all the other variables that distinguish us from each other.

When you think about the meaning of a text or of an event, you have to carefully consider whether you mean the factual mean-ing, the explanatory meaning, or the interpretative meaning.

FRAMEWORKS

It is not possible to analyze the latent content of a text without looking at it through some *analytic framework.* An analytic framework is some system for organizing or making sense of data. The purple monstrosity Barney, for example, can be seen in a number of different ways. With a conservative framework, Barney can be seen as a liberal Trojan Horse trying to brainwash children with notions of love, noncompetitive interaction, and self-esteem issues. From a Marxist perspective, Barney can be seen as one of the more blatant examples of corporations under-mining authentic culture and turning children into consumers. From a business framework, Barney can be seen as an attempt to increase profits and can be evaluated as either successful or un-successful. From a fundamentalist Christian point of view, Barney's antics might be evidence of the media's secular humanist values.

Which view of Barney is "true"? This question makes no sense because it assumes that one of the frameworks is correct or that a researcher need not use any framework at all—and neither of these assumptions is true. There is no *meaning* to Barney apart from that which can be generated by looking at Barney in some sort of context. The context is provided by the analytic frame-work.

This use of analytic frameworks makes the analysis of latent content very difficult. If you remember, in the beginning of this book I said that the point of research methods was to enable you to convince people who were not predisposed to agree with you. In the case of content analysis, this can be extremely difficult if two people are using competing analytic frameworks. The only lesson to be learned from this is that you must be as open as possi-ble in your assumptions, as clear as possible in your conceptual-izations and operationalizations, and as persuasive as possible in your writing and data presentation.

RELIABILITY AND VALIDITY

The question of reliability is usually countered with assertions about validity. The question of reliability comes up because of the difficulty in operationalizing concepts in a medium that contains visual, audio, and linguistic text. As the examples given in this chapter have shown, the difficulty frequently seems insurmount-able. It is this problem in operationalization that drives content researchers into a more qualitative methodology. But the payoff in terms of validity that one usually gets in qualitative analysis does not materialize in this case because the researcher is dealing with latent content.

The question of validity arises in another way as well, and this pushes the researcher deep into philosophical and theoretical quandaries. The researcher wants to say that the text *is* a certain way or *says* certain things, but that assumes that there is an objectively obtainable latent meaning *regardless of who is receiving the text.* There may very well be an objectively obtainable meaning, but it is impossible to say that people actually receive this meaning if one is looking only at the text. This is a *unit of analysis* problem: You cannot look at the meaning *sent* (the text) and draw conclusions about the meaning *received.* To do that, it would be necessary to study the audience and not the media.

Figure 9.1 illustrates the possible *locations* of the meaning of a text. All three "locations" are accepted both by common sense and in media scholarship. The first box indicates that one definition of meaning involves the producer's (speaker's, writer's) intention. So if you want to know what something means, you have to figure out what the producer intended. Instead of asking, for example, "Do Americans have a constitutional right to bear arms?" you would ask, "Did the writers of the Constitution mean that private individuals had the right to own weapons for private purposes?" The meaning of the Bill of Rights, from this view, depends on the *intentions* of the authors. On the other hand, some would argue, the Bill of Rights is written down in black and white, "in plain English." In this case, we are dealing with the center box in Figure 9.1, and the text "speaks for itself." This view is the literalist's view, and whether one is talking about the Bill of Rights, the Bible, or a story in the *Washington Post,* it is a very difficult position to maintain. At its most sophisticated, it does not shun all interpretation; rather, it restricts the interpretational context to the document (or media product) in question. It operates hermeneutically, using the whole to explain the parts and the parts to explain the whole. Finally, there is the third box. This box represents what is called *reception theory.* Here, what is important is what the text means to the audience. The right to

Figure 9.1. Locating Meaning in Texts

bear arms in the United States cannot possibly refer to the right to own muskets—even if muskets are what the Founding Fathers had in mind—because the weapons we are concerned with are contemporary weapons (as muskets were once contemporary). Reception theorists see message reception as *a meaning-making process* rather than as a passive, purely receptive one.

Content analysis deals primarily with the middle box, using approaches ranging from the literalist perspective to hermeneutic analysis. Imagine that you are studying television programs from the late 1960s and have chosen *Bewitched* and *I Dream of Jeannie* as your examples. (Let's imagine that these shows are typical of that decade's programming to avoid starting a discussion of sampling. Sampling will be discussed in the next section.) You conclude that the programs had a profoundly ambivalent attitude toward women. In both programs, the women are more powerful than the men. In both programs, the men are domineering and controlling. Whereas the male star in *Bewitched* is basically a mean-spirited dullard who is trying to protect the traditional family, the male star in *Jeannie* is primarily trying to protect his job. Both of the men, however, would be much happier if the women did not have magical powers.

You cannot conclude from this that "Americans'" or "society's" values about women were profoundly ambivalent. You do not have any data concerning Americans or "society." Both of these programs, like many of the programs during the turbulent 1960s and 1970s, contained two possible "readings." On the one hand, these programs could be easily and consistently understood as being about women's oppression by the male patriarchal, rational-logical social structure. The women's power in these programs was based in nonrational traditions repeatedly described as older (and obviously more effective) than those of the men. The relationship the women had with the men, however, required that the woman acquiesce to the man's perspective.

On the other hand, these programs were about irrational women who continuously put the male's achievements in jeopardy. Both of the men were successful, and neither of the women worked. The women's misunderstanding of the work world, as well as their basic irrationality, continuously threatened to cost the men their livelihood.

Both shows could also be put into a modernity versus tradition framework, but the analysis gets really complicated. Jeannie and Samantha both base their abilities on premodern traditions, whereas the men (an advertising executive and an astronaut) reflect very modern ways of thinking. The men are also "rational," whereas the women are not: In *Bewitched* the rationality works against the man, but it works in the man's favor in *Jeannie*. Of course, Jeannie's Captain Nelson is a "real" man (handsome, virile, military), whereas Samantha's Darin is a wishy-washy incompetent. Darin was so inconsequential that when the original actor died, he was replaced and no one seemed to mind. Nelson was the perfect symbol of modernism in that he combined rationality, science, and the military. Darin, on the other hand, desperately wanted to maintain his idea of a traditional marriage, whereas his wife, the witch, wanted to move into a more equal relationship. Nelson didn't want to be married at all. You can see, that if your analytic framework is modernity/tradition, you will have to tease out different relevant themes (rationality, for example, and power or equality). A change in focus results in a change in research results.

The objective description of the interaction between the characters and of the recurring themes in the programs can show us these possible readings, but it cannot determine *how the programs were actually perceived by the audience*. Because of this, the question of validity is very tricky in content analysis. And, as is repeatedly stated in this chapter, this means that the content analysis researcher—like the field researcher—must be as open, honest, and lucid as possible.

More on Generalizing Beyond the Texts

We stated earlier that content analysis generally restricts the interpretational context to the document or media product in question and does not generalize beyond it. But there are two exceptions to this rule. First, we can consider the mass media texts as synonymous with the culture. For example, we might say that American culture is violent because American media content is violent. In this case, we would be *not* be saying that American *society* is violent: We would be drawing a distinction between American society and American culture, recognizing that it is possible to have a violent culture in a relatively nonviolent society. The conclusions that we draw about the culture do not imply that people in that society think or act a certain way.

Not everyone is willing to consider mass media texts as synonymous with the culture; the extent to which they are depends on how one defines *culture.* We are on surer ground when we generalize from the mass media to "popular culture" because popular culture and the mass media are generally seen as overlapping, if not synonymous, concepts.

The second exception involves texts that are not from the mass media. Mass media content is produced by a corporation and is designed to be consumed by anonymous and diverse members of an large audience. If, however, we were looking at literature produced by and for survivalists, we would be on much stronger ground when arguing that the content represented the thinking, feelings, or values of both the producer and the audience. The argument would not be automatic, but a single author (or a very small group of authors) and a specific, targeted audience would make getting evidence much easier. If the material were constantly reprinted or if there were requests from a variety of survivalist groups, we could conclude that an analysis of the text would be an analysis of the people producing and consuming it.

SAMPLING

Sampling is crucial to all forms of content analysis. As mentioned above, if you are going to be discussing content that is not immediately apparent, the burden of proof will be on you. You are going to have to show that you didn't just look at those texts that could best support your argument.

For example, if you want to discuss the relatively weak roles that women have in films, you cannot mention only those films in which women have weak roles. You must choose a *sample* that represents a *population,* which means in this case that you must select films that are representative of the kind of films you are talking about. It is necessary to clearly define the population of films with which you are concerned. Are you interested in the relatively weak roles that women have in limited-release art films, in popular films, in films aimed at teenagers, in adventure films, in films since 1980, or in comedies? If you are interested in popular films in general, then you have to specify if you mean *successful* films (operationalized, perhaps, as films that had box office receipts in the top 20 in the year of release) and the time period (*all* films or films in a certain era).

The sampling should be random or systematic to the extent that this is possible. Once you have decided what your population is going to be, you must figure out a way of sampling from within that population in such a way that all of the texts within the population have an equal chance of being included.

Sampling is crucial because we all have *impressions* of media content based on our own idiosyncratic selections. As a researcher, you have to overcome these impressions. A good sampling design is one of your most persuasive tools.

One of the problems with sampling is having a sampling frame—a list of potential "subjects" from which you can choose.

Fortunately, some sources allow access to almost complete universes of content from which samples can be drawn. The on-line database Lexis-Nexus is an excellent source of news stories in newspapers, magazines, and selected television news programs. The Internet Movie Data Base (www.imdb.com) provides an exhaustive list of films, both foreign and domestic and both cinematic and made for television.

THE VARIABLES

I define content analysis as any research methodology that centers on the analysis of content. Not everyone does this. Some writers think of content analysis as entirely a quantitative activity, with more qualitative approaches being labeled something else: *explication du texte,* for example, or *semiotics,* or *cultural studies.*

Obviously, as we know from the discussion of fieldwork, the more qualitative one's research is, the less sense it makes to speak of variables. In content analysis, however, because the burden of proof is so high, it is really imperative to think in terms of variables—and operationalization—as much as possible. This does not mean that all content analysis must be quantitative, but it does mean that all content analysis must be as empirically sound as it can be made—and it must be recognized that the extent to which it is not possible to be empirically sound is exactly the extent to which people are free to dismiss your ideas.

So, going back to our example of weak roles for women in modern movies, it would be necessary to treat roles as a variable. Then we would have to operationalize what a "weak" role is and how it is distinguished from a "strong" role. It might be necessary to add a definition and operationalization of "moderate" roles as well. We would also have to operationalize what it means to be a "woman in modern movies," and this implies that we would be able to say what it means to be a "man in modern movies" as well. Unless men and women are compared, we cannot make any statement about women's roles. The reason we would have to define what is meant by a "woman in modern movies" is that there are so many people in films who really don't have roles at all—all those *background* people, the waitresses and pedestrians and shop clerks. Should we count them or not? It is up to you. It depends on your question. But to be empirical, you have to decide *in advance,* and that is why the variable-analytic tradition needs to be drawn on, if not explicitly used.

A good example of the use of operationalization in a qualitative content analysis occurs in Edward Armstrong's (1993) analysis of violence in pop music lyrics. Although it is a media commonplace that rap music has violent lyrics, other forms of music have not come under the same scrutiny. Armstrong looks at rap and country western music and compares them for violent content. Armstrong ignores rock and roll because "in rock, the music is more important than the words" and because rock fans rarely understand the words in the songs (p. 67). In rap and country, Armstrong claims, "content is central" to the music (p. 67).

Armstrong operationalizes violent lyrics as any lyrics that deal with murder, manslaughter, or assault. He then develops two dimensions of violence: physical prowess and masculinity. The analysis is qualitative, so the operationalization is loose:

> Toughness is a focal concern represented by a compound combination of qualities. First among these is physical prowess. [A] "tough guy" is hard, fearless, undemonstrative, and skilled in physical combat. The second component is called "masculinity." Included here are a conceptualization of women as conquest objects and a concern over homosexuality often accompanied by violent physical attacks. (pp. 72-73)

This operationalization is completed through the use of examples. Johnny Cash's line "I shot a man in Reno just to watch him die" is an example of prowess. It shows that he can kill a man casually, for no reason. On the other hand, "She's naked and I'm a Peeping Tom. Her body's beautiful so I'm thinking rape" puts one Geto Boys' rap into the masculinity category: women as objects of conquest. Whether or not you think killing people is a sign of prowess or that rape is a sign of masculinity, Armstrong's operationalizations let you know how he is using the word. They let you know what he is doing *empirically*.

Units of Analysis

The weakness of the variable-analytic treatment that needs to be recognized is that the more clearly you define and operationalize a concept, the more nuance you lose. In content analysis, an overly rigid application of the variable-analytic tradition has a tendency to destroy the very thing you are trying to get at: meaning. This will be clear if we discuss the idea of a *unit of analysis.*

The *unit of analysis* in a study is the actual thing you are measuring. The important thing to remember about units of analysis is that you can draw conclusions about things at the *unit level* (and larger, if you are careful), but you cannot draw conclusions about anything smaller than the unit level. An example will help.

You can study businesses in a number of ways. You can

- Look at businesspeople—their values, motivations, and abilities
- Study individual businesses—the way they are positioned in the market, the types of marketing strategies they use
- Study industries—the conditions under which they grow and decline, the way they are affected by shifts in currency values, the way they respond to labor pressures

In the first case, the unit of analysis is individual people involved in business; in the second, it is individual businesses; and in the third, it is industries. You cannot study businesses and draw conclusions about individuals. General Motors, for

example, was best described for years as sluggish, slow to inno-
vate, and top heavy, but this does not mean that the individuals
who worked there were fat, dull people with large heads. In the
same way, what you can say about the computer industry may not
apply to individual companies. The rule about *units of analysis* is
that you must be very careful about what you are actually gathering data about and then *not go beyond your data.*

The problem with the variable-analytic tradition in content
analysis is that it tends to gravitate toward units of analysis that
are too small: single words or scenes, individual characters or actions. It is much more useful to think in terms of the hermeneutic
circle, that the meaning for the whole text is created out of all the
units from which it is made *and* the meaning of all the smaller
parts is derived from the complete picture.

So although the use of variables is crucial in persuasively analyzing texts, a loose usage is required if the meaning of the text is
not to be destroyed. One has to be particularly aware that, as in
real life, cultural texts are suffused with meaning. Thus, one cannot simply count scenes of violence or sex, for example, because
sex and violence within texts have meaning, a purpose: What
is the *point* of the violence? Is it to show the evil nature of
some character? Or is it to illustrate that the hero has the ability
to fight for certain principles? Is it ironic or humorous or gratu-
itous? If there is sex, what is the context? Is it love, flirtation,
friendship, rape, brutality, or something else? And what is the
function of the love, flirtation, friendship, rape, or brutality
within the story?

I stress the use of variables, despite their inherent problems, because of the need for operationalization. Sex and violence, two
perennial pop culture concerns, for example, are notoriously difficult to operationalize without reducing them to mechanical descriptions of physical movements. And no matter what else sex
and violence may be, they are not reducible to purely physical descriptions. Unless there is some operationalization, there really is
no progress beyond impressions. Remember, the point of re-

SIDEBAR 9.3 A Reminder About Terminology

The variable-analytic tradition was discussed in the chapter on variables. This tradition approaches research with the idea that the reality being studied can be reliably and validly broken down into variables, generally variables that can be reduced to a numerical value. This tradition is contrasted with a more narrative approach to explanation, such as that found in history and in anthropology. The variable-analytic approach is known as the *nomothetic* approach, and the narrative approach is called *ideographic*.

search methodology is to convince people who may be predisposed to disagree with you.

VISUAL AND VERBAL ANALYSIS

Content analysis tends to focus on the print media or to reduce nonprint media to printlike texts. Television news, for example, is often analyzed using transcripts of what was said, and the visual and audio elements are almost entirely dropped. The analysis of music lyrics just discussed is a good example of this.

It is possible to analyze the visual and audio elements of a media production, but it is just much more difficult to do so—and especially difficult if one is using a quantitative analysis technique. We know that the expressions that are used and the tone of voice employed can change the meaning of a remark in ways both subtle and profound, but it is extraordinarily difficult to operationalize expressions or tones of voices. Think of irony as an example. An ironic statement is often identified only by an accompanying ironic expression or tone of voice. The statement itself is simply a factual remark or an opinion, and it is quite likely that a transcript would lose the irony altogether. We know this—but how do you operationalize the concept "ironic expression"?

Descriptions of camera angles and lighting can be used, but they tend not to be. I think that multimedia presentations will be able to vastly expand our ability to analyze visual and audio content.

WRITING

The key to writing content analysis is to enable the reader to see what you are talking about. In this way, writing content analysis is much like writing fieldwork. This is the case even if you are using a primarily quantitative method. In a qualitative analysis, the ability to visualize must be incorporated into the discussion of data. The discussion of data must include lots of examples and certainly examples of all of your key points. In a qualitative content analysis, you should use examples in the operationalization phase so that the reader knows exactly what you are counting.

Keep in mind that latent content is not obvious and that a given framework is neither immediately clear nor necessarily shared. This is an interpretative science, and you are frequently trying to make people see commonplace things in a new light. Respect the positions of the readers. Remember, the burden of proof is on you.

COMMENTS

Ethical Considerations

Content analysis rarely raises ethical issues. This is because, for the most part, content analysis is associated with texts rather than with people. And the texts that communication scholars—especially mass media scholars—like to examine are already part

SIDEBAR 9.4 Vocabulary

Manifest content	Latent content	Text
Analytic frameworks	Unit of analysis	

of the public domain. This means that generally questions about coercing or misleading subjects are outside of the scope of this sort of analysis.

However, as I've already argued in the earlier "Comments" sections, content analysis can also be used in other methodologies such as fieldwork and survey research. In these cases, the ethical considerations of those methodologies are extended to content analysis. In content analysis, texts are analyzed using frameworks that, quite often, are foreign to both the producers and to the audience. This is not a problem when the texts are fashion ads for women and the framework is Marxist feminism. It can be a problem when you are analyzing the comments of members of a small group and conclude that their *latent* message is a negative one (racist, for example, or sexist or cultist). Quite often, members of these small communities feel that they can be individually identified (at least by insiders), and they are concerned with how they are perceived by outsiders.

When using content analysis in research projects that are shaped primarily by another methodology, you need to be aware of the ethical pitfalls of that methodology.

Other Considerations

This has already been mentioned, but it needs to be emphasized. Content analysis of mass media products cannot directly tell you what the producers or the audience think, feel, or value. This sort of analysis, of course, can be a part of an argument about the way people think, feel, or value, but you need data from something beside the content itself. It is tempting, especially when dealing with fringe elements, to draw conclusions about the producers and/or the audience, but it is really difficult to do so with the content of the commercial mass media.

ACTIVITIES AND EXERCISE

1. Think about prime time television commercials and the different frameworks that you could use to analyze them. What questions would you think could be asked from a Marxist perspective? From a feminist perspective? From an ethnicity perspective?
2. If you wanted to study magazine advertisements, how would you create your sample? First think of a research question, and then describe your sample.
3. How would you design a study to look at news bias? Take the position that you are a conservative Christian and think that the media are liberal and secular. How would you study this?

APPENDIX A

List of Journals

Argumentation and Advocacy
Communication Education
Communication Monographs
Communication Quarterly
Communication Reports
Communication Research
Communication Studies
Communication Theory
Critical Studies in Mass Communication
Howard Journal of Communication
Human Communication Research
Journal of Applied Communication Research
Journal of Broadcasting and Electronic Media
Journal of Communication
Journal of the Association for Communication Administration
Journalism Quarterly
Philosophy and Rhetoric
Quarterly Journal of Speech
Southern Communication Journal
Text and Performance Quarterly
Western Journal of Communication

APPENDIX B

Reading for Fieldwork:
John Sumser's Close Encounters:
Gender and the Use of Public Space[1]

Ideas from Carol Gilligan's *In a Different Voice* and Erving Goffman's *Relations in Public* are used to inform a field study of the use of space in a small snack bar in Pennsylvania Station in New York City. The differences between the way the males and females used the limited available space were both profound and entertaining. The single female customers were quite open to interaction and formed a great many transitory, single-sex groups. The male customers who came in alone used perceptual blinders to maintain—and respect—privacy and remained alone though their stays.

Carol Gilligan's book *In a Different Voice* is an attempt to develop the idea that men value autonomy and individuality whereas women value relationships and, to a degree, selflessness. According to Gilligan, these values translate—or should translate—into separate, gender-specific ethical systems. Whether or not these kind of ethical conclusions can be drawn, Gilligan's work does raise the possibility that we can discuss separate, gender-specific mores. To examine the idea that men and women have radically different views of what constitutes normal and reasonable behavior, I decided to observe the interaction of strangers in a public place. Pennsylvania Station in New York City was chosen as the field study area because strangers meeting in a transportation center are unlikely to attempt to establish long-term bonds.

Much of Erving Goffman's work concerns the interaction between strangers in public places. In his *Relations in Public* (1971), Goffman discusses waiting rooms and the problems involved in trying to adapt ideas of "personal space" to an environment with a fluctuating population. Notions of personal space in waiting rooms tend to be flexible due to frequent changes in the number of people using the space. This means that when entering a waiting area normal notions of private space go into suspension if the area is fairly crowded. "Obviously, to stand or sit next to a stranger when the setting is all but empty is more of an intrusion than the same act would be when the place is packed and all can see the only the niche remains" (p. 31). Goffman goes on to say that awkward situations arise when one sits next to a stranger if the reason for the acceptability of the intrusion is removed—if, that is, one sits immediately next to a stranger only to have the room empty moments later. This problem is exaggerated, according to Goffman, if the individuals involved in the situation are of opposite sexes: The intruder will feel that more distance should be created but will also wonder if it is not even more offensive to pick up and move away. With all this in mind, we can look at the interaction at Pennsylvania Station.

Most of the eating establishments on the commuter level in Pennsylvania Station in New York City have counter service rather than table service. The restaurants that do have table service are generally nearly empty, whereas the counter service snack bars are extremely busy most of the day. Among these snack bars Le Café stands as an anomaly: It is clean. It is thoughtfully designed with bright white walls, exposed brickwork, and blond wood tables and counters. Le Café specializes in cakes and coffee but also serves ice cream, chili, pita bread sandwiches, and soft

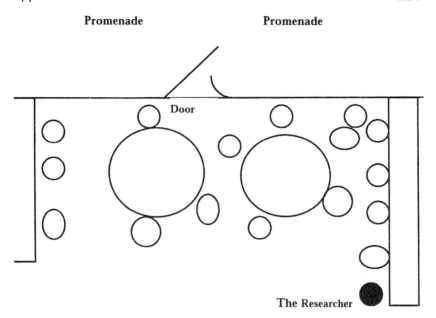

Figure B.1. Diagram of Le Café

drinks. It has two things in common with its competitors: It is there not so much to feed people as to serve people who use food and drink as a means of passing time, and it is too small to seat all its customers. Le Café has the potential to seat 16 people. The actual seating capacity varies according to how the customers have rearranged the stools. At the time of this study, there was seating available for 14. The two extra stools were jumbled in among the stools along the west wall. The stools are of the drafting table type, and the tables and counters are correspondingly high. What are here referred to as the east and west counter are actually shelves about 14 inches wide that are attached to the brick walls. Between these counters are two tables about 1 yard in diameter (Figure B.1).

The customers of Le Café can be divided between those who buy food to take out and those who buy food for consumption on the premises. Because there are 14 available stools and only four eating surfaces (the two tables and the two counters), much of the time anyone seeking a seat must sit at a location that is already being used. This study is the history of one of those tables between hours of 3:00 and 4:45 on a Friday afternoon. Illustrations will be drawn from the activity of the other table and from the counters.

The Russian Countess spoke as much with her eyes and fingers as with her mouth. Her jeweled fingers flashed from the darkness of her thick, black wool coat as her story led the Lady in Gray from garage sale to antique restorer to insurance appraiser. The Lady in Gray was perhaps 15 years older than the Countess and looked like a grandmother who was resting comfortably at the top of some career ladder or other at Macy's or Bloomingdales. She listened intently to the Countess. Both had long finished their pastry and were nursing the probably cold remnants of their coffee. They had not come in together and did not know one another.

Both nodded politely to the Doll Woman as she tried to get on a stool without dropping her cake, coffee, purse, paper sack, and large, clear plastic bag of colorful cloth dolls. The Doll Woman lived in Central Islip and traveled into New York once a week to sell her handsome dolls on street corners in Manhattan. She had been doing this only since her husband died, at which time she realized that she was 62 years old and that sewing was her only marketable skill. She was dressed in a ill-matched, ill-fitting assortment of clothes and had a soft round face and gray hair tucked loosely into a bun atop her head. Almost immediately the eyes and fingers of the Countess included the Doll Woman in the conversation. The Lady in Gray shifted her position so that she was now obliquely, rather than directly, facing the Countess, which indicated that although she was aware that the Countess was the center of focus, the Doll Woman was also part of the group. Soon the Countess's story was finished, and a conversation developed around the events that she had related. All three participated equally, although the Countess remained dominant because it was her story that had generated the discussion and she was frequently called upon to clarify points.

Just about the time the story was finished, the Girl say down. The Girl was casually dressed in corduroy slacks and wore a crewneck sweater over a blue shirt with a Peter Pan collar. She was about 27 years old. As she sat down, she looked at the three other women, and they looked at her. The conversation expanded to include the Girl, although she remained silent throughout her stay. She followed the conversation with her eyes and changed her expressions often enough to indicate that she understood what was being said. It was obvious, however, that she did not understand the background for the remarks being made, which is probably why her participation was not more active. A few times it looked as if she were going to drop out of the group by lowering her eyes to her plate, but each time she was brought back in— twice by the Countess (who at one point went so far as to touch the Girl's hand) and once by the Lady in Gray and the Doll Woman.

The Girl was the first to leave, which she did half-apologetically. Everyone at the table said good-bye to her. This leave-taking broke the group solidarity, and everyone shifted around in their seats, slowly gathered things together, and finally exchanged phone numbers. The Countess and the Lady in Gray exchanged cards; the Doll Woman wrote down her number on a bit of napkin and gave it to the Countess, who in turn gave the Doll Woman her card. The Doll Woman said that she came to the city only once a week, and the Countess told her, "Oh, call me at home. Please feel free to call at my home." The Doll Woman left. The Countess and the Lady in Gray walked out together and, with much squeezing of elbows, parted in the promenade.

The table was dormant for about 7 or 8 minutes. It was cleared and wiped. The ashtrays were neatly repiled on the top of the napkin dispenser, and the salt and pepper shakers were briskly realigned. The stools remained where the four women left them.

A young black woman, referred to here as Glasses, sat down facing the promenade, arranged her coffee and cake, opened her book, and began reading. She was in her late teens or early 20s and wore dark pants and a bright, bulky sweater. A minute or so after she sat down, three identical young men (the Boys) boisterously piled on to the remaining stools. They appeared to be on a coffee break from one of the local shops. All three had light brown hair and wore white shirts rolled up and various versions of red ties and brown pants. Glasses looked at them a few times, then settled down to read. The Boys never looked at her, and after about 10 minutes Glasses left. The Boys bullshitted rather than talked, saying things like, "That jerk!" and "You fool." They asked questions of each other that were never answered such as, "What time is it?" and "Whacha doin?" They moved about on their stools only to remount a moment later. One of the Boys left the table to get in line to buy an ice cream.

Perhaps 5 minutes after Glasses left and just as the one Boy went to get ice cream, a white woman about 22 years old sat down at the table. This woman also wore glasses. Her hair was pulled back and held in place with two blue plastic clips. She looked as if she belonged in Vermont: She wore blue jeans, walking shoes, and a oatmeal-colored rag sweater that had most likely come from an L. L. Bean catalog. This outfit was set off by an alarmingly incongruous shade of neon lipstick. She had a pita bread sandwich full of cheese and sprouts, and as she ate she continuously watched the Boys. The Boys studiously ignored her. Sprouts would look abstractly at the newspaper she had in front of her, take a bite of her sandwich, then watch the Boys as she chewed. The Boys never once made eye contact with her. This bizarre charade lasted approximately 15 minutes. The Boys never ceased to bullshit, never ceased their almost constant movement, and never once in any way acknowledged the fact that Sprouts was sitting at their table. The Boys finally left at the instigation of the ice cream eater. Sprouts left shortly after, and once again the table was vacant.

The lipstick worn by Members Only meshed well with her high consumer fashion. She carried a designer bag (brown with designer names all over it) and wore high-heeled shoes and very blue, very tight Brooke Shields jeans. Her face was made up as an exact duplicate of someone else's. It took her a while to sit down because she was rummaging in her designer bag (looking, perhaps, for her *Cosmopolitan* magazine), and by the time she was ready to sit down another woman was already perched on a stool, watching her. This second woman was a dramatic 40 or so with lots of black hair who dressed much the same way as did Members Only. As she climbed up on her stool, Members Only said something to the other woman, and the other woman responded. These two had quite a conversation. They both leaned across the table and spoke seriously in low voices. This lasted more than 20 minutes. They left together and stood talking just outside the door of Le Café for a minute or two before walking off in different directions. Just as these two were leaving, two businessmen came in together, ordered coffee, and sat at the table just vacated by Members Only and her new friend. These men stayed for perhaps 5 minutes, then left.

During the time all this was happening at the west table, the east table was enjoying a similar progression.

. . .

Both the male and female customers of Le Café carried reading material. The men who came in alone read what they had brought; the women at the tables simply placed the material in front of them. The one exception to this was a woman who read while her table was occupied by a couple who were engrossed in one another. As soon as this couple left, however, the Reader fell back into the female pattern of looking only absentmindedly at her book while spending most of her time looking at other customers. She soon became deeply involved in a conversation with a woman in her early 60s, and the book was totally ignored. It is interesting that while this conversation was going on a third woman (in her late 20s) sat down at the table and began flipping through a magazine while following, absently, the conversation. She sat like this for perhaps 15 minutes. Finally the Reader left, and before she was out the door, the older woman and the magazine flipper were embroiled in a conversation that lasted 12 minutes. The magazine flipper left, and the older woman stayed until her table was occupied by two men in ties who had come in separately and who spoke to, and acknowledged, no one.

Reading material served very different purposes for the males and females who came into Le Café. Reading material was carried by the men to be read. If it served any social function at all, it was to isolate the reader and to create a bit of private space in a very public place. But in any case, it *was* read. Reading material carried by women seemed to be used as an excuse to sit down. It was as if they were saying, "I'm not butting in. I'm just going to read for a bit." Though all the women seemed to want to talk, and most ended up talking, none of them simply plopped down with a "Well, what's going on here?" attitude. At the same time, because the reading material was not actually being read, there was no danger of anyone feeling that they were interrupting. The two women who came in *in order to read* sat at the counters with their stools angled away from the surrounding people. These women would have had to have been interrupted to start a conversation, and no one made any attempt to do so.

The men say at the tables only if there were no stools available at the counters or if they had come in as part of a group or a couple. The women, on the other hand, sat at the counters only if there were no open stools at either of the tables. For the two women who came in separately and were forced by lack of table space to sit at the east counter, the same pattern of skimming reading material followed by conversation took place.

The men preferred wedging themselves into uncomfortable counter seats even when there was space available at one of the tables and even when one or both of the tables were vacant. The men who were forced to sit at one of the tables due to lack of counter space made no eye contact with anyone. The extreme instance of this occurred when the Reader had the table momentarily to herself (just prior to the arrival of the older woman) and all the counter seats were taken. A man in his mid-30s placed his briefcase on a stool at the Reader's table and his pastry and coffee cup on the table top, and *stood* eating and drinking and looking at the wall. His entire stay (after receiving his food) lasted less than 3 minutes and was the shortest stay I observed.

The lack of eye contact made by the males was nothing short of amazing. If one were to have made brief film clips of the men in Le Café there would be no indication that there were other humans around. Similar film clips of the women would have enabled the viewer to *count* the surrounding people. There were two instances when men who were seated at counters took napkins from tables occupied by one or two females and the existence of the females was never recognized. In one case, an older man wrestled with a too-tight napkin dispenser for perhaps 30 seconds directly in front of a watching female (again, the Reader), who had to move her coffee to made room for this invasion. The older man focused solely on the napkin dispenser, the woman only on the man.

In contrast to the men, the women nodded or smiled at anyone who sat at their table, and these nods and smiles were always returned by other women. (Men, of course, never saw them because they never looked at the women.) These nods fitted with the books, magazines, and newspapers in that they simply indicated that the tables were now being shared by another person who was also passing time. At this point, conversation could or could not begin without a sense of either abruptness or rebuff. Conversation did not so much start among the women as it was eased into without any sudden, startling, or contrived transition.

Gilligan's theory that men and women have very basic value differences and that these differences have created separate patterns of evaluating behavior can be seen if we accept that neither the men nor the women were rude. Both the men and women were scrupulously polite, but polite in totally different ways. Politeness for the women consisted in establishing contact in very subtle, comfortable ways. Politeness for the men consisted in not infringing on another's privacy. This was taken to absurd lengths in the napkin incidents and in the situation involving the Boys. These male examples can be contrasted with the interchange between the Countess, the Lady in Gray, and the Doll Woman, on the one hand, and the Girl, on the other. The Girl was included even though she was really too late to take part in the conversation. The women recognized everyone; the men, no one.

To say that the men were socially inept or that the women were a particularly gregarious lot would be to miss the seeming pervasiveness of the differences. Goffman's view that personal space needs to be flexible in places such as waiting rooms seems to be correct, but his analysis may be, in light of Gilligan, overly "male." The women in Le Café did not feel the awkwardness that Goffman discussed and that the men in Le Café apparently experienced. The men were trying to juggle notions of autonomy and privacy in a context that left little room for either. The women, already leaning toward relationships rather than individual autonomy, actually profited from the breakdown of any overly rigid idea of private space.

An alternative explanation to that of social "paradigms" is potentially much simple, but fails to account for all that transpired in the restaurant. It could be that the men had just finished working or were on breaks (they all wore ties) and that the women were in town, alone, shopping. There is no way to know this because women can dress up to shop much as they dress to work. They do not have badges such as ties that indicate employment. The fact that both the Countess and the Lady in Gray had cards indicates that they were probably employed. Because of this uncertainty in dividing the male and female customers into workers and nonworkers, any explanation in terms of the loneliness of the long-distance shopper cannot be justified.

NOTE

1. Paper presented at the annual meeting of the American Sociological Association, September 1986.

REFERENCES

Arendt, H. (1963). *Eichmann in Jerusalem: A report on the banality of evil.* New York: Viking.

Armstrong, E. G. (1993). The rhetoric of violence in rap and country music. *Sociological Inquiry, 63*(1), 64-81.

Barnes, B., Bloor, D., & Henry, J. (1996). *Scientific knowledge: A sociological analysis.* Chicago: University of Chicago Press.

Barthel, D. L. (1984). *Amana: From pietist sect to American community.* Lincoln: University of Nebraska Press.

Beatty, M. J., & Behnke, R. R. (1991). Effects of public speaking trait anxiety and intensity of speaking task on heart rate during performance. *Human Communication Research, 18*(2), 147-176.

Beatty, M. J., McCroskey, J. C., & Heisel, A. D. (1998). Communication apprehension as temperamental expression: A communibiological paradigm. *Communication Monographs, 65*(3), 197-119.

Beniger, J. (1983). Does television enhance the shared symbolic environment? Trends in labeling of editorial cartoons, 1948-1980. *American Sociological Review, 48,* 103-111.

Beniger, J. R. (1986). *The control revolution: Technological and economic origins of the information society.* Cambridge, MA: Harvard University Press.

Brown, J. D., Dykers, C. R., Steele, J. R., & White, A. B. (1994). Teenage room culture: Where media and identities intersect. *Communication Research, 21,* 813-827.

Browning, L. D., & Beyer, J. M. (1998). The structuring of shared voluntary standards in the U.S. semiconductor business: Communicating to reach agreement. *Communication Monographs, 65*(3), 220-243.

Buller, D. B., LePoire, B. A., Aune, R. K., & Elroy, S. V. (1992). Social perceptions as mediators of the effect of speech rate similarity on compliance. *Human Communication Research, 19,* 286-311.

Camden, C. T., & Kennedy, C. W. (1986). Manager communication style and nurse morale. *Human Communication Research, 12,* 551-563.

Collingwood, R. G. (1962). *An essay on philosophical method.* Oxford, UK: Clarendon.

Coppleston, F. (1960). *A history of philosophy: Vol. 6. Modern philosophy* (Part 2). New York: Image.

Crossen, C. (1994). *Tainted truth: The manipulation of fact in America.* New York: Simon & Schuster.

Dindia, K. (1987). The effects of sex of subject and sex of partner on interruptions. *Human Communication Research, 13,* 345-371.

Duneier, M. (1999). *Sidewalk.* New York: Farrar Straus Giroux.

Entin, K., Aly, N., Sumser, J., & Giventer, L. (1997). *Strategic directions: A needs assessment and industry targeting analysis of Stanislaus County.* Modesto, CA: Stanislaus County Economic Development Corporation.

Fadiman, A. (1997). *The spirit catches you and you fall down: A Hmong child, her American doctors, and the collision of two cultures.* New York: Farrar Straus Giroux.

Finz, S. (1998, May 23). Santa Clara County angry over report: Officials say state crime study skewed. *San Francisco Chronicle* [Online]. Available: http://sfgate.com/cgi-bin/article.cgi?file=/chronicle/archive/1998/05/23/MN80389.DTL

Fire from the sky. (1998, May 7). *The NewsHour with Jim Lehrer.* Transcript available from NewsHour Web site, www.pbs.org.

Fumento, M. (1998, August). "Road rage" versus reality. *Atlantic Monthly,* pp. 12-17.

Gaines, D. (1998). *Teenage wasteland: Suburbia's dead end kids.* Chicago: University of Chicago Press.

Geertz, C. (1973). *The interpretation of cultures.* New York: Basic Books.

Giles, H., Henwood, K., Coupland, N., Harriman, J., & Coupland, J. (1992). Language attitudes and cognitive mediation. *Human Communication Research, 18,* 500-527.

Greenberg, B. S., & Brand, J. E. (1993). Television news and advertising in schools: The "Channel One" controversy. *Journal of Communication, 43*(1), 143-151.

Halle, D. (1984). *America's working man: Work, home, and politics among blue-collar property owners.* Chicago: University of Chicago Press.

Harper, D. (1987). *Working knowledge: Skill and community in a small shop.* Chicago: University of Chicago Press.

Kim, M.-S., & Wilson, S. R. (1994). A cross-cultural comparison of implicit theories of requesting. *Communication Monographs, 61*(3), 210-235.

Kuhn, T. S. (1970). *The structure of scientific revolutions* (2nd ed.). Chicago: University of Chicago Press.

Lang, G. L., & Lang, K. (1983). *The battle for public opinion: The president, the press, and the polls during Watergate.* New York: Columbia University Press.

Leis, W. (1972). *The domination of nature.* New York: George Braziller.

Liebes, T. (1988). Cultural differences in the retelling of television fiction. *Critical Studies in Mass Communication, 5,* 277-292.

Lippmann, W. (1922). *Public opinion.* New York: Penguin.

Loh, E. S. (1993). The economic effects of physical appearance. *Social Science Quarterly, 74*(2), 420-438.

Milgram, S. (1974). *Obedience to authority: An experimental view.* New York: Harper & Row.

Morse, R. (1998, June 2). Back to school on shootings. *San Francisco Examiner,* p. A2.

Polanyi, M. (1962). *Personal knowledge: Towards a post-critical philosophy.* Chicago: University of Chicago Press.

Postman, N. (1993). *Technopoly: The surrender of culture to technology.* New York: Knopf.

Secter, B. (1995, November 5). The "science" of made-to-order statistics: Slyly comparing apples and oranges often rationalized as serving a higher cause. *San Francisco Examiner,* p. A2.

Sobel, R. S., & Lillith, N. (1975). Determinants of nonstationary personal space invasion. *Journal of Social Psychology, 97,* 39-45.

Sumser, J. (1986, November). *Close encounters: Gender and the use of public space.* Paper presented at the annual meeting of the American Sociological Association, New York.

Trujillo, N. (1992). Interpreting (the work and the talk of) baseball: Perspectives on ballpark culture. *Western Journal of Communication, 56,* 350-371.

U.S. Bureau of Labor Statistics. (1995, August). *How the government measures unemployment: Labor force statistics from the current population survey* [On-line]. Available: http://stats.bls.gov/cps_htgm.htm

Vangelisti, A. L., & Crumley, L. P. (1998). Reactions to messages that hurt: The influence of relational contexts. *Communication Monographs, 65*(3), 173-196.

Weigery, A. (1994). Lawns of weeds: Status in opposition to life. *American Sociologist, 25*(1), 80-96.

Weitzel, A., & Geist, P. (1998). Parliamentary procedure in a community group: Communication and vigilant decision making. *Communication Monographs, 65*(3), 244-259.

When it comes to men's mugs, softer is sexier: Women attracted to feminine faces. (1998, August 27). *San Francisco Chronicle,* p. A3.

Wilson, B. J., Linz, D., Donnerstein, E., & Stipp, H. (1992). The impact of social issue television programming on attitudes toward rape. *Human Communication Research, 19,* 179-208.

Wittgenstein, L. (1968). *Philosophical investigations* (3rd ed.). New York: Macmillan.

Wood, P. B. (1993). Book review of *Who is black? One nation's definition* by F. James Davis. *Sociological Inquiry, 63,* 243-245.

Yam, P. (2000, January). Mammal melee: New fossils impugn leading model of early mammal origins. *Scientific American,* p. 25.

Zussman, R. (1985). *Mechanics of the middle class: Work and politics among American engineers.* Berkeley: University of California Press.

INDEX

ABOUT THE AUTHOR

J ohn Sumser has two degrees in philosophy and a doctorate in sociology. He is currently a Professor and Chair of the Department of Communication Studies at California State University, Stanislaus, which is located in Turlock, California. He has a novel currently under consideration at a major publishing company and is also working on a book looking at the impact of communication technology on social theory and philosophy.